Please Pass the Biscuits, Pappy

Number Eight

Clifton and Shirley Caldwell Texas Heritage Series

PLEASE PASS THE BISCUITS, PAPPY

Pictures of Governor W. Lee "Pappy" O'Daniel

Bill Crawford

Introduction by John Anderson

University of Texas Press

Austin

Publication of this work was made possible in part by support from Clifton and Shirley Caldwell and a challenge grant from the National Endowment for the Humanities.

First edition, 2004

Requests for permission to reproduce material from this work should be sent to Permissions, University of Texas Press, P.O. Box 7819, Austin, TX 78713-7819.

∞The paper used in this book meets the minimum requirements of ANSI/NISO Z39.48-1992 (R1997) (Permanence of Paper).

Crawford, Bill, 1955–
    Please pass the biscuits, Pappy : pictures of Governor W. Lee "Pappy" O'Daniel / Bill Crawford ; introduction by John Anderson. — 1st ed.
        p.   cm, — (Clifton and Shirley Caldwell Texas heritage series ; no. 8)
    ISBN 0-292-70575-1 (alk. paper)
    1. O'Daniel, W. Lee (Wilbert Lee), 1890–1969—Pictorial works.   2. O'Daniel, W. Lee (Wilbert Lee), 1890–1969.   3. Legislators—United States—Biography.   4. United States. Congress. Senate—Biography. 5. Governors—Texas—Biography.   6. Texas—Politics and government—1865–1950. 7. Musicians—Texas—Biography.   I. Title.   II. Series.
E748.O33C73   2004
976.4'063'092—dc22
                                                                                                    2003026028

Contents

Acknowledgments

The authors would like to acknowledge the following individuals who contributed to this project: Chuck Bailey, indefatigable collector of political Texana; Cary Ginell, whose Origin Jazz Library (www.originjazz.com) provided valuable factual and audio information concerning O'Daniel's recording history; Mel Brown and John Hauser, for services above and beyond the call of duty; Brenda McClurkin at the University of Texas at Arlington; Gene Fowler and the wonderful staff at the Border Radio Research Institute; Harry Kieke, for his insight into photography at the Department of Public Safety; Kathy Lane, Joe Tisdale's daughter; Jeff Rowe and his crew at Austin Prints for Publication, John Carrico, Maria Hansen, Dundee Murray, and Ruth Weaver; Penelope Dukes-Williams with the Legislative Reference Library; and Tom Shelton and Dolores Olvidarez at the University of Texas at San Antonio Institute of Texan Cultures; and the creative and hard-working team at the University of Texas Press. Finally, we would like to thank the dedicated and knowledgeable staff of the Archives Division of the Texas State Library and Archives Commission.

Please Pass the Biscuits, Pappy

Introduction

Governor W. Lee O'Daniel and the
Texas Department of Public Safety Photo Archives

JOHN ANDERSON

Likenesses of all the men and women who have served Texas as governor are among the hundreds of thousands of images related to Texas, Texans, and state government in the Prints & Photographs Collections of the Texas State Archives.[1] Sam Houston was the early photographer's dream subject, constantly affecting new appearances and costumes, from jaguar vests to cowboy dusters. The portly Governor Hogg perched on a wide tree stump, begging irreverent comparison to a bullfrog, and even Ma Ferguson allowed a somber pose or two. James Allred openly enjoyed the glamorous company of Ginger Rogers and other Hollywood stars.

Preston Smith took glee in inviting his favorite country-western performers and his beloved little granddaughter into the picture. The otherwise stodgy Bill Clements was a good sport who enjoyed some laughs at the expense of his loud sport coats and reputedly stalled a bill signing until the normally fastidiously punctual photographer Bill Malone arrived.[2]

Ann Richards engineered a photo opportunity featuring her special edition Harley Davidson, with "Born to Be Wild" blaring in the background. (She either learned from Michael Dukakis's mistake[3] or simply had her own good sense to hold the helmet custom-painted "Gov Ann" in her hands rather than pulling it over her famous "big" hairdo.) But, to date, it is Wilbert Lee "Pappy" O'Daniel who decidedly had more fun in front of the camera than any other Texas governor.

For a great state in the depths of a Great Depression, things were really starting to happen in Texas in the 1930s. Grand preparations were underway for celebration of the 1936 centennial of the Texas Revolution and the founding of the Republic of

Pappy O'Daniel pretending to be talking on the telephone while working at his desk in the Capitol. This photo is one of several included in the album presented to Governor and Mrs. O'Daniel from Joel Tisdale and the employees of the DPS, Christmas of 1939. (Texas State Library and Archives Commission #1976/8-150)

Texas. The people who were known to make things happen in Texas had been talking about it since 1923, the Texas Centennial Board of One Hundred met in Austin in 1924 to start planning, and the Texas Centennial Commission came into being ten years later.[4] Of three cities nominated as sites for an elaborate exposition, Dallas won the prize. The Centennial was going to be a big deal, and nothing, not even a Great Depression, was going to get in the way.

In anticipation of the Centennial, plaques were erected and historic sites commemorated at dusty roadsides all around Texas. The graves of heroes were located and marked (in some cases, even if that meant exhuming their remains and re-interring them in what were believed to be more suitable sites.)[5] Photographers roamed the state documenting the vestiges of its vanishing early architecture.[6] The young men of the Civilian Conservation Corps (CCC) built parks and facilities for people to enjoy, and the Works Progress Administration (WPA) and related New Deal programs tackled a variety of other improvements.

In 1936 the state was busy publishing the first set of official county highway maps. By June of that same year, the Texas Highway Department had constructed fourteen snapshot-perfect, staffed information stops around the state, each built to reflect the architectural materials and style of the region. They were among the first permanent tourist bureaus in the United States.

Texans were in a frenzy of exploring their diverse heritages and cultures and geographies for themselves and exporting the facts, the stories, and the legends and myths to the outside world. But if Texans were to rediscover their own heritage and non-Texans to come and partake fully of the largest state, they had to be able to get around. The condition of many Texas roads and highways was abysmal and, due to burgeoning private automobile and commercial truck traffic, severely inadequate and growing profoundly hazardous. The concern was not a new one—the Texas Good Roads Association[7] had promoted the improvement of the state's dirt and gravel roads and highways since the early part of the century. To compound the problem, enforcement of traffic laws and license and weight restrictions ranged from spotty, to lackadaisical, to nonexistent in Texas.

The year the U.S. economy began its collapse, 1929, was also the year that saw the Texas Highway Patrol, by legislation, organized within the Texas Highway Department. The original Patrol was minuscule in comparison to the immense

Pre-DPS Highway Patrol motorcycle officers assembled on the Capitol drive. The woman standing at the left of the patrol officers was an office employee assigned to the unit. The photo was made by the commercial studio of Jordan-Ellison of Austin. (Texas State Library and Archives Commission #1983/112-P-1-A)

breadth of Texas it had to cover. Though the Patrol's manpower and authority expanded significantly in 1931, only with the legislature's creation of the Department of Public Safety commission in 1935 was there renewed hope that Texans could travel the state's roads and highways safely and that traffic laws could be enforced effectively and uniformly.[8]

The Texas Department of Public Safety, the DPS, was an agency just getting into gear when O'Daniel became governor in 1937, but in many ways it had hit the road rolling. The Texas Rangers, previously under the Texas Adjutant General's Office, entered a welcome new era of ethical and professional law enforcement as a division of the DPS. There were a crime lab and forensics, there were training and education, there were modern vehicles and tools and techniques, and modern communications. Precisely when is uncertain, but the department employed photographers soon after its formation. The Texas State Archives holds DPS photos dated as early as 1937, and some undated ones that may have been made earlier. To date, the photographic records of the DPS have come to the Archives in several accessions from 1976 to 1983 and include tens of thousands of extraordinary images.

At the DPS the primary applications for photography were forensics, documentation, education, and training. The photographers were also charged, more and more through the years, with public information and promotional work. In fact, a great number of the later DPS images transferred to the State Archives seem to have been made to promote the public image of the Highway Patrol, Texas Rangers, and other divisions.

On May 5, 1937, a twenty-seven-year-old photographer, Joel Tisdale, left the Austin Police Department to work for DPS.[9] Not long after, Tisdale was assigned to the governor's detail.[10] The arrangement must have worked. A beautifully crafted, tooled saddle-leather album of sepia-toned photo prints was presented to Governor and Mrs. O'Daniel by the employees of the Texas DPS at Christmas of 1939.[11] Beneath the dedication on the title page appears "Photographs by Joel Tisdale."

While research is by nature never ending, Joel Tisdale is believed, at this writing,

Unidentified photographer covering the receiving line at a Governor's Mansion reception O'Daniel held for Texas legislators. Lieutenant Governor and Mrs. Coke Stevenson are at the left of the line, headed by Governor and Mrs. O'Daniel. The photographer is probably reaching for a flashbulb or sheet-film holder in his coat pocket. Who is the DPS photographer photographing the photographer? (Texas State Library and Archives Commission #1976/8-31)

The DPS photographers developed comfortable relationships with O'Daniel's family. Son Pat experimented with various portrait poses at the Mansion. Here he smiles broadly for the camera, October 1940. (Texas State Library and Archives Commission #1976/8-169)

to have made most of the DPS photos in this book. Many others are probably the work of his colleagues, but as there are no other specific attributions, we regret that we are not able to credit them.

Photographing the activities of the governor in the early years of the DPS would have been an understandable, even obvious inclination and a natural outgrowth of its task of providing transportation and security for the chief executive of the state. Open to question is whether the impulsive and media-savvy Governor O'Daniel noticed the DPS snapping a few photos, discovered the department operated a photography section, and in his straightforward and unabashed manner requested a shooter or, conversely, the DPS administration thought it would be a politically expedient move to actively court the governor's vanity.

Whatever the exact dynamics and sequence of events, Governor O'Daniel eagerly put these photographers to work, at taxpayer expense, documenting his activities, including daily life at the Governor's Mansion, his ambitious road trip visits with Texas legislators, his outlandish inaugural barbecue preparations, his daughter Molly's wedding, and campaigning for re-election as governor and for election to the United States Senate. Ironically, at the same time O'Daniel was happily exploiting a variety of DPS resources, including cars, an officer-driver, and photographers, he was vetoing appropriations for the Narcotics Section of the DPS and curtailing funding for other activities.[12]

The economic and sociological events of the 1930s set the stage for great experiments with publicly funded photography programs. It is hard to say to what degree the DPS administration may have been aware of programs such as Roy Stryker's at the federal Farm Security Administration (FSA), launched in 1937, or to what extent the DPS photographers were familiar with the work of

Is Pat O'Daniel frowning or puzzled? (Texas State Library and Archives Commission #1976/8-170)

JOHN ANDERSON

The DPS officer assigned to O'Daniel dressed in a patrolman's uniform. The officer served as the governor's driver and security. Pappy poses with the military rifle he used to shoot a buffalo for his inaugural barbecue. On the radio he characterized it as an "old musket." (Texas State Library and Archives Commission #1976/8-62)

Ready to head out on a car trip, the officer driver, Merle and Governor O'Daniel, and photographer Tisdale pose with the 1940 Ford "Fordor" sedan under the Mansion's porte-cochere. The 1940 Ford was an affordable, instant classic, and was the next to the last model put out before World War II interrupted auto production. A product of the Depression, the flathead V-8s first introduced in 1932 powered Fords into the 1950s. The reliable and reasonably fast Fords of this era were favorites of both cops and robbers. (Texas State Library and Archives Commission #1976/8-720)

contemporaries such as Alan Rothstein, Dorothea Lange, Margaret Bourke-White, Walker Evans, or Russell Lee. What can be said is that photography was in the air.

Tisdale and his colleagues assuredly did not see themselves as sociologists, social or political propagandists, artists, nor even as photojournalists.[13] Regardless of how Tisdale and the other DPS photographers viewed their mission, they were highly capable and took pride in their craft. They committed the occasional compositional faux pas (see page 79, where O'Daniel appears to be wearing a funny little cap that is actually the porch lamp), as well as the universal error of making double or multiple images when they forgot what they were doing and exposed the same sheet of film more than once. But, interestingly and to their credit, even some of their most obvious mistakes remain in the files—these were government records.

The DPS photographers accomplished some of what the 1930s social-experiment photographers did, if with entirely different motivation. Certainly what they achieved was a lot more than "good enough for government work," as the disparaging expression goes.

After the long-awaited birth of the DPS in 1935, most of its operations headquartered at Austin's historic Camp Mabry, as had its main predecessor organizations, the Adjutant General's Office and the Highway Department. The camp, named for former Adjutant General Woodford H. Mabry, was founded in 1892, and at this writing is one of the oldest active military installations in Texas.[14]

At the beginning of the twenty-first century, Camp Mabry, with its woods, water, rolling landscape, and open spaces in the heart of central West Austin, is considered prime real estate and thus in perennial jeopardy. In the early 1930s it was in the pastoral extreme northwest quadrant of the city. Its immediate state neighbors according to a 1933 city map[15] were, in the terminology of the time, "The State Deaf, Dumb and Blind Institute for Colored" to the northeast on Bull Creek Road and "The State School for Defectives" to the south. The County Poor Farm was farther to the south and the State Insane Asylum was a good ways to the east, near Hyde Park, Austin's first, boldly planned suburb.

Though the old post's perimeter has been strengthened and the security heightened after 9/11/2001, the Camp opens its gates to a daily stream of civilian visitors who come to walk, jog, bicycle, visit the Texas Military Forces Museum, or simply enjoy the open spaces it affords.

Once Buildings #10 and #11, as they are now designated, housed the DPS headquarters, crime lab, classrooms, shooting range, and, from 1935 to 1952, presumably the photo lab and photography section. These two historic buildings were originally built in 1918 to serve as barracks for the Air Service School of Automobile Mechanics, a wartime collaborative project of the United States Army and the University of Texas. In 1937 the two buildings benefited from practical and aesthetic amenities created by the WPA. In fact, a number of WPA projects in the distinctive rustic CCC style survive at Camp Mabry, including the guard post, stone wall, and stone pyramids.[16]

> If you are puzzled about the kind of camera to buy, get a Speed Graphic . . .
> for two reasons . . . it is a good camera, and moreover it is standard equip-
> ment for all press photographers . . . cops will assume that you belong on
> the scene and will let you get behind police lines.
>
> WEEGEE [ARTHUR FELLIG][17]

As Arthur Fellig, the legendary New York freelance crime photographer known as Weegee, asserts, the Speed Graphic was de rigueur for anyone truly serious about making photographs—and that included cops and, down in Texas, the Department of Public Safety.

The Speed Graphic, first introduced in 1912, was one of the most successful of an extensive line of cameras manufactured by the Folmer and Schwing Company (an outgrowth of a nineteenth-century bicycle-manufacturing concern) and its several successors. The "Speeds" made from 1912 to 1927 were known as "Top Handle" models. In 1928 the handle was moved to the side of the camera for obvious ergonomic reasons and, more significantly, the camera was engineered to accept a greater range of lenses.

The Speed Graphic is the camera that we see in the photos on pages 7 and 13. One model has the curved wire-hoop viewfinder characteristic of the "Pre-Anniversary" model manufactured from 1928 to 1939.

The "Anniversary" model of the Speed was introduced in 1940,[18] so it is theoretically possible that Tisdale could have used one in the last part of the O'Daniel administration. Later cameras were available with an optional revolving back, so that the photographer could select a vertical or horizontal composition without turning the camera. But this was not an option with Tisdale's early camera. It had a stationary back—meaning that horizontal format was the fixed default—so the whole camera had to be turned 90 degrees to get a vertical picture.

When Harry Kieke signed on as a photographer in July 1971,[19] the department had already been in its new headquarters on Lamar Boulevard for a number of years, but the photographers were still using essentially the same 4×5 inch sheet-film press camera technology that Joel Tisdale and his colleagues had been using in the late 1930s and the 1940s.

By the time Kieke came on board, the Speed Graphic had been largely replaced by the Crown Graphic model that debuted in 1952. Despite the semantic connotations, the Crown was actually lighter, simpler, and more versatile than the Speed. Kieke, assigned to forensics, was the photographer who was on call twenty-four hours a day to go to the scene of a serious crime anywhere in Texas by whatever means could get him there the quickest. Obviously needing to streamline his work process, Kieke pioneered the shift away from sheet film to medium format Mini-Graphics with 120 roll-film adapter backs, and eventually to 35mm single-lens reflexes, using his own Topcon model to demonstrate its speed, economy, and utility. Still active in photography at age eighty-five, long after his retirement from the DPS, Kieke has made the switch entirely to digital photography well before many of his younger counterparts.

The cameras that Tisdale and his counterparts employed early on used only sheet film—4×5 inches was the standard. The Department also used 8×10 cameras, mostly back at headquarters, seldom in the field, and certainly not for travel or capturing quick-moving events. A few of the photos in this book (e.g., p. 58) were printed from 8×10-inch negatives and as a result are incredibly sharp images, even sharper than those made from the "large-format" 4×5s.

Sheet film photography (which is still used today for many applications) has a whole regimen unfamiliar to the point-and-shoot casual photographer of our times. Unexposed film was loaded into a sheet-film holder that was then slipped into the back of the camera. One holder accommodated two sheets of film, one front and one back—yielding two shots. You got your picture plus an extra if you needed it. After the first sheet was exposed, the dark slide had to be reinserted (preferably coded correctly to indicate that the film had been exposed). The holder was removed from the camera back, flipped over, and reinserted. Then the dark slide was again removed, the shutter cocked, and you were ready to go. The veteran photographer could do this with amazing speed, but the technique is a far cry from popping in a 36-exposure cassette of 35mm film. With a current motor-driven, autofocus camera, the photographer can burn 36 frames in a matter of seconds.

For a long road trip, the abundantly resourced photographer could load dozens of holders in advance. Or, more likely, film could have been carried in the manufacturer's original light-proof boxes and loaded into the film holders either in the convenience of the darkroom or in a changing bag. Loading film required deftly feeling

An unidentified man behind the scenes at Molly O'Daniel's wedding reception at the Governor's Mansion, July 31, 1941, is perplexed by the flashbulbs in the mixer. The mixer was probably the first convenient receptacle the photographer found to corral the loose bulbs. These powerful #2 screw base bulbs were made by the Wabash Company of New York. The Speed Graphic camera on the table has the curved wire-hoop finder characteristic of the Pre-Anniversary models made through 1939. (Texas State Library and Archives Commission #1976/8-231)

for the manufacturer's code notch and sliding the sheet in under the holder's runners, all the while being careful not to scratch the film, before replacing and locking the dark slide. Even in mild heat and humidity, loading a quantity of sheet-film holders in a changing bag can be tedious, uncomfortable, and exhausting.

During Tisdale's career, innovations improved on the two-sheet holder and made film changing more convenient. These included roll film adapter backs, multi-sheet Grafmatic film holders, film packs, and readyloads. In fact, a few images in the book were captured on 3×4-inch film packs, but this was not common during the O'Daniel administration.

Loading and changing film was one part of the process. Providing enough light for the exposure was another critical part. One of the reasons that the DPS images in this book look so good is that most of the views were illuminated by flashbulb. Flashbulb illumination was not only used indoors, where there may not have been enough available light, but was especially used outdoors, synchronized with daylight to eliminate harsh shadows.

First introduced into the United States about 1930, flashbulb light is often described as a softer, rounder illumination than modern electronic strobe can produce. Flashbulbs were available in a wide array of types and sizes and typically provided much more illumination than the on-camera electronic flash of today. For all the advantages of flashbulbs, however, they were single use—the bulb had to be replaced for each and every new exposure. The bulbs were large, fragile, and cumbersome to carry. The powerful Wabash #2 flashbulbs that we see in the humorous photo made at the Governor's Mansion had screw bases just like household light bulbs.

> But there is a kind of power thing about the camera. I mean everyone
> knows you've got some edge. You're carrying some slight magic which does
> something to them. It fixes them in a way.
>
> DIANE ARBUS[20]

O'Daniel had a way of turning a quick photo opportunity into a party. The resulting photos are not only testimony to O'Daniel but also to the photographers who covered him. But what about all the people pictured in these photos? As we study the photos we see that they represent a broad spectrum of Texas society. While many of the subjects seem to enjoy some affluence, many others are not in the best of circumstances. Yet, for the most part, the people seem happy to be photographed. Certainly part of that willingness would simply have been the novelty of being visited by a governor and photographed with him, and added to that was O'Daniel's considerable measure of charisma and enthusiasm.

But another possible part of the equation was that these people had been through a lot during the Depression and they wanted to feel good about something, to be included in something important. Having the handsome, well-dressed photographer of the governor pay attention to you by focusing his imposing camera outfitted with a formidable flashgun specifically on you probably filled the bill.

State ethicists would throw up their hands and run off screaming if today's standards were applied to all of O'Daniel's misuses of privilege and resources. (And misappropriation of DPS photography resources paled in comparison to his many other abuses.) Today his use of DPS photographers to cover his campaigns and his daughter's wedding would be glaring ethics violations. But therein lies the paradox. The fact that he did so widely document his abuses of power, on camera, provides us with a unique portrait of his administration, to the delight of archivists and historians.

Before the Department of Public Safety photographers began documenting the governor and other state activities, there was little, if any, officially prescribed photography. News photographers and local commercial studios shooting on speculation might cover events (as in the photo on page 5), but there was no provision for methodical, long-term preservation of the images created. Examples of these photos survive today in the State Archives and other collections, but the DPS photos of O'Daniel are unique in that the images are government-created photographic records destined for archival posterity. More than thirty years later, the establishment of the Senate Media, House Photography, and the Archives Current Events programs at the advent of the 1970s helped to further ensure a photographic chronicle of Texas state government.[21]

Recent governors have been careful to use nonpublic funds and nonstate photographers to document their activities. The unfortunate, and paradoxical, loss to the public is that the visual documentation of these administrations once again remains under the proprietary control of the photographer or the entity that hired her or him.

During the period of the late 1930s and the 1940s, the major film manufacturers—Kodak, Agfa, and others—were struggling to produce a "safety" film that would not be as dangerously flammable as the cellulose nitrate–based film (commonly known as "nitrate") that had been in use for decades. As a result of accelerated research and development, the manufacturers marketed a variety of films that were cellulose diacetate based.

*The O'Daniel Christmas
tree in the Mansion was
included in the 1939 album.
Governor George W. Bush
selected this historical photo
for his 1999 Christmas card.
(Texas State Library and
Archives Commission
#1976/8-155)*

Cellulose diacetate film addressed the problem of flammability, but the base often proved to be dimensionally unstable over time. As manufacturers experimented and changed formulations, some batches would remain stable for decades and others warped and buckled relatively soon. Translating to another medium and or freezing the original negatives are ultimately the only practical known means of forestalling the destruction of the images.

At the Texas State Archives much work has been done to save hundreds of the original DPS negatives, but many more thousands of images remain vulnerable for lack of adequate funding. While the DPS photo archives benefit from the climate control, fire suppression, and security offered by the State Archives, there are no easy solutions to ensure survival of the photos.

The photos in this book are fleeting instants from a unique time in the history of the people of Texas fixed precariously in the material realm. I invite you to look closely, study the places, revel in the faces, learn, question, and enjoy.

NOTES

1. "Texas State Archives" is the informal name for the Archives and Information Services Division of the Texas State Library and Archives Commission. Tracing its colorful roots back to the Republic of Texas, the Archives is charged with collecting, preserving, arranging, describing, and making available the permanently valuable records of Texas history and government.

2. Senate Concurrent Resolution 114, 1969, resolved to study an appropriation for photographing state government events for the Archives. Bill Malone served as the current events photographer for the Texas State Archives from 1970 to 1991.

3. The political fortunes of presidential candidate Michael Dukakis were thought by some observers to have further soured after he donned a tank commander's bulbous helmet for a photo op.

4. *Handbook of Texas.*

5. The remains of several prominent Texans were dug up and reburied at other sites in the early 1930s. This was a movement that may be traced to as early as 1913, when the remains of Johanna Troutman, the Betsy Ross of Texas and a native of Georgia who never visited Texas in her lifetime, were exhumed and reburied at the State Cemetery.

6. Fannie Ratchford, a University of Texas librarian, traveled the state in her car and photographed antebellum homes and other structures. Her work is collected at the Texas State Archives, Prints and Photographs #1970/101. A federally funded program, the Historic American Building Survey (HABS), employed skilled professional photographers to document buildings across the United States.

7. *Handbook of Texas.*

8. James W. Robinson, *The DPS Story* (Austin: Texas Department of Public Safety, 1975), pp. 6 and 9. The legislation also strengthened enforcement of criminal laws.

9. Joel Tisdale obituary, *Austin American-Statesman,* February 7, 1984.

10. Interview with Chuck Bailey, former general counsel for the DPS, from recollections of the late DPS photographer Wallace Nelson.

11. The 1939 Christmas Album (#1987/173-26) is included in the records of Governor W. Lee O'Daniel, Texas State Library and Archives Commission.

12. Robinson, *DPS Story,* p. 19.

13. Some attribute coinage of the term "photojournalism" to Wilson Hicks, circa 1952, others to Cliff Edom, dean of the School of Journalism at the University of Missouri. In any case, the word was not a familiar term during the O'Daniel era.

14. *Walking Tour of Camp Mabry* (Texas Adjutant General's Office).

15. Texas State Library and Archives Commission, Archives Map Collection Map #925, "Map of the City of Austin," Austin Chamber of Commerce, November 1933.

16. *Walking Tour of Camp Mabry.*

17. Weegee [Arthur Fellig], *Naked City* (Essential Books, 1945), p. 240 (reprint, New York: Da Capo Press, 1975).

18. The term Anniversary was used to designate the fiftieth anniversary of the Folmer and Schwing Company being in business manufacturing cameras. While various models of Graflex and Graphic cameras were made from the 1890s to the 1970s, the actual ownership of the company changed several times.

19. Telephone and personal interviews with Harry Kieke, 2003.

20. *Diane Arbus: An Aperture Monograph* (Millerton, NY: Aperture, 1972), p. 13.

21. House Photography and Senate Media were created and in place for the 1971 legislative session.

Wilbert Lee "Please Pass the Biscuits, Pappy" O'Daniel

An Appreciation

BILL CRAWFORD

They've come to town with their guitars,
And now they're smoking big cigars—
Them hillbillies are politicians now.

CAMPAIGN SONG WRITTEN BY W. LEE O'DANIEL FOR HIS 1938
TEXAS GUBERNATORIAL CAMPAIGN

The film *O Brother, Where Art Thou?* (Touchstone Pictures, 2000) introduced audiences to the character Menelaus "Pass the Biscuits, Pappy" O'Daniel, the governor of Mississippi, a back-slapping politico who campaigned over the radio and rode into office on the melody of a hillbilly song. While audiences enjoyed the fictional character as portrayed by screen veteran Charles Durning, the story of the real Pappy O'Daniel was even more amazing.

Like a bottle rocket whistling against the North Texas sky, the arc of W. Lee "Please Pass the Biscuits, Pappy" O'Daniel's political career was startling, flashy, and brief. O'Daniel was a songwriting flour salesman who launched the career of country music legend Bob Wills. Within four years, O'Daniel won two elections for governor and two for U.S. senator, defeating Lyndon Baines Johnson in Johnson's first Senate race. O'Daniel was a Texas version of Arnold Schwarzenegger, a media superstar who became an electoral terminator. What made Pappy's ballot-box muscle even more amazing than Arnold's was that he was an Ohio-born Republican sympathizer in an all-Democratic state who wasn't even registered to vote when he launched his first political campaign.

From our twenty-first-century perspective, it is almost impossible to imagine what life was like in the Lone Star State in 1938, when isolated Texas farm families thrilled to the voices coming out of the Grebe or Aeriola radio set in the living room, and the promise of a million-dollar smile could boost a flour-selling political novice to the state's highest political office. There has never been a Texas politician quite like Governor W. Lee "Please Pass the Biscuits, Pappy" O'Daniel, and there will never be one like him again.

From 1938 to 1942, O'Daniel won the hearts, if not the minds, of Texas. Supporters hailed him as "the miracle man of Texas politics."[1] "He's a good man," declared one supporter. "He's almost a preacher."[2] Critics vilified him as a "dubious messiah of rainbow chasers in a state that has lived under six flags and a flour sack"[3] or as "a fiddling carpetbagger from Ohio"[4] who offered Texans nothing more than "whangdoodle music, flapdoodle poetry, and doodlebug statecraft."[5] Brief and controversial though his career was, O'Daniel's creation of a conservative Christian pro-business political persona and his brilliant use of the broadcasting media were profoundly prescient. In many ways, the modern era of Texas politics, the era of hi-tech mass media campaigns and massive Republican victories, traces its roots back to the honey-voiced radio homilies of W. Lee "Please Pass the Biscuits, Pappy" O'Daniel. As he announced shortly after winning his first gubernatorial race, "This next administration is not going to be me and God—it is going to be by God, the people and me. Thanks to radio."[6]

Wilbert Lee O'Daniel was born on March 11, 1890, to poor farming parents in Malta, Ohio, near the banks of the Muskingum River. When Wilbert was still a toddler, his father was killed while working on a construction project. Soon after his father's death, O'Daniel's hard-working Church of Christ mother married an old friend, a widower with two children of his own. The blended family moved to the plains of central Kansas and began a new life together on a tenant farm outside the town of Arlington.

O'Daniel grew up a church-going farm boy, a bright overachiever. After graduating from high school, he opened and operated a restaurant. He sold the business, cleared $100, and used the money to pay for his tuition at the Salt City Business College in Hutchinson, Kansas. He finished the two-year course in eight months and took a job as the stenographer for a salesman at a local flour-milling concern.

It was the perfect niche for the ambitious, bright O'Daniel. By age twenty-seven, he was a partner in his own company, the Independent Milling Company. On June 30, 1917, he married fellow Salt City graduate Merle Estelle Butcher. The

O'Daniels moved to Kingman, Kansas, where their first son, Pat, was born on December 4, 1918. By 1920, the Independent Milling Company had gone bust, and O'Daniel had taken a position with the United States Milling Company in Kansas City, where his son Mike was born on March 29. By the time daughter Molly was born on Valentine's Day 1922, the O'Daniels had moved to New Orleans. After the United States Milling Company also failed, the peripatetic salesman moved his family to Fort Worth, Texas, on July 4, 1925. There, he took a job with J. Perry Burrus, owner of the Burrus Mill and Elevator Company, makers of Light Crust Flour.

In the 1920s and 1930s, flour milling was big business, as most Texas women baked their daily bread. In 1937, milling ranked fourth in the value of manufacturing statewide, behind petroleum refining, meatpacking, and the manufacture of cottonseed oil and cottonseed cakes.[7] Though the oil industry was introducing big business to the state, Texas was still largely rural and largely poor. Texans lived in a "colonial economy." Their livelihood came primarily from Texas crops, livestock, minerals, and other raw materials that were purchased by manufacturers outside the state, turned into products, and resold to Texas consumers. Of the state's total 1937 population, 59 percent lived in rural areas and communities with populations of less than 2,500. The state was also predominantly white. Anglos made up 73.5 percent of the population, blacks 14.7 percent, and Hispanics 11.7 percent.[8]

O'Daniel quickly made a place for himself in the Fort Worth business community. The young salesman reaffirmed his church-going roots and joined the Magnolia Christian Church. He altered his name, going by W. Lee instead of Wilbert. To some, he explained that the name Lee was given to him by his mother in gratitude for a Doctor Lee who attended his birth in Ohio. To others, he explained that the name Lee came from the wish of an uncle, a Yankee soldier wounded during the Civil War, who wanted to show his gratitude to the Confederate family that had nursed him back to health.[9]

O'Daniel boosted sales of Light Crust Flour by overcoming his Texas customers' prejudice against products manufactured in Texas. O'Daniel explained to all who would listen that Texas flour had "high protein content" and enjoyed a "favorable comparison with any other flour." Sure enough, O'Daniel's efforts dramatically increased flour sales, and he was promoted to president of the Fort Worth mill.

In 1931, six years after O'Daniel's arrival in Fort Worth, Truett Kimzey, an engineer and part-time announcer at Fort Worth radio station KFJZ, introduced O'Daniel to the magic of the airwaves. Broadcasting was far from a proven marketing device at that time. Television was nonexistent. KFJZ was one of only three radio stations in Fort Worth, small enterprises struggling to compete with the three daily newspapers for ad dollars. The most powerful radio station in town, WBAP (We Bring A Program), was founded and owned by Amon Carter, publisher of the *Fort Worth Star-Telegram* and Fort Worth's flamboyant front man. KFJZ was a low-power station, only 150 watts, owned and operated by the Meacham family, who also owned the H. C. Meacham Company department store in Fort Worth.

Kimzey met with O'Daniel and explained to him that the Aladdin Lamp Company had withdrawn their financial support for the broadcasts of the Aladdin Laddies, a trio of local musicians including singer Milton Brown and a fiddle player and part-time barber by the name of Bob Wills. The Laddies broadcast from Kemble's Furniture Store in downtown Fort Worth. The musicians liked the arrangement because it gave them ample opportunity to learn the latest popular tunes from the store's stock of newly released records.

Kimzey suggested to O'Daniel that Light Crust Flour would be a perfect sponsor for the Laddies. Owner Will Ed Kemble, who was an acquaintance of O'Daniel, also put in a good word for the boys. After some hesitation, O'Daniel reluctantly agreed to the proposition, on the condition that he would not pay anybody anything until the program proved its worth.

Wills and the band started their 7 A.M. broadcasts in January 1931 from the KFJZ studios—described by one observer as "nothing more than the back room of Meacham's store." A few hundred radios within fifteen miles of the station's transmitter heard an assortment of fiddle tunes, including "21 Years" and "The Chicken Reel." Truett Kimzey announced the program and read ad copy for Light Crust Flour written by O'Daniel. After a few days, either Kimzey or Bob Wills, or both, jokingly referred to the band as the Light Crust Doughboys, the name that the band uses to this day.

At first, KFJZ didn't receive any more response to the Doughboys than to the Banjoneers, Uncle Dudley and Marguerite, or any of their other performers. Unimpressed, O'Daniel fired the band. For a few weeks, the band played over the radio without a sponsor. Finally, Wills went to talk to O'Daniel himself. The fiddler waited in the Light Crust Flour offices for two days before getting an audience with O'Daniel. After listening to Wills plead his case, the flour salesman magnanimously offered to sponsor the radio program once again if the band members worked a forty-hour week at the flour mill in addition to playing on the radio every morning. The band tried this for five weeks before deciding that they had had enough of millwork at $7.50 per week. Luckily, the station was getting a good response to the show

by that time, and O'Daniel agreed to sponsor the radio program and allow them to quit working at the mill, as long as they practiced music for eight hours a day. The band happily agreed to the new arrangement.

O'Daniel was still not sold completely on the program and told the band that he did not like their "hillbilly music."[10] What the Light Crust Doughboys actually played was a sophisticated blend of jazz, blues, and fiddle tunes that would eventually come to be known as western swing. Their music was a hot, danceable, and cheery sound that appealed especially to women. And women were the ones who bought flour.

Word of the program began to spread. Ever-growing audiences eagerly awaited the bright, cheery announcement "The Light Crust Doughboys are on the air!" O'Daniel continued to write all the ad copy. He also began to compose little poems and songs, which were included in the show. In March 1931, he rented a bus, decorated it, fixed it up with a loudspeaker, and sent the band to a baker's convention in Galveston. The success of that appearance inspired O'Daniel to buy a custom-outfitted seven-passenger Packard for the band and book them for numerous live appearances. On one occasion the band was scheduled to go on a goodwill tour with the Fort Worth Chamber of Commerce. At the last minute, announcer Truett Kimzey could not make the trip, and O'Daniel decided to take his place.

Weatherford, Texas, was the first stop. As O'Daniel stepped up to the microphone, the crowd sized up his thick chest, his impeccable grooming, and his easy smile. They listened attentively to his soothing baritone voice, clear and rich, with a down-home yet formal drawl. It was soon obvious that the audience really liked O'Daniel, and O'Daniel really liked being in front of an audience. According to another version of the story, it was Wills who invited O'Daniel to the KFJZ studios and encouraged him to say a few words on the air.[11]

However it happened, O'Daniel was bitten by the broadcasting bug, and he took over as the announcer for the Light Crust Doughboys. By October 1931, Pappy was paying for airtime out of his own pocket, a half-hour for $10.[12]

O'Daniel moved the Light Crust program from low-powered KFJZ to Fort Worth's 10,000-watt WBAP, and he changed the time of his daily broadcast to 12:30 P.M., just in time to entertain Texans at their noontime meal. Tired of traveling around the state to appear on different stations, O'Daniel helped to set up the Texas Quality Network in 1934. One of the first statewide broadcasting networks, TQN distributed O'Daniel's program on a "chain" of stations that included WOAI in San Antonio, WBAP in Fort Worth, WFAA in Dallas, and KPRC in Houston.[13] Leon McAuliffe remembered walking three blocks from his home to the store while a teenager in Houston and "never missing a word of a song. In the summer every window was open and every radio was tuned to the Light Crust Doughboys." When O'Daniel wanted to add a Hawaiian sound to the Light Crust musical mix, he invited McAuliffe, who played the steel guitar, to join the band.

As their fame increased, the Light Crust Doughboys received numerous offers to play lucrative shows in clubs like the Crystal Springs Ballroom, a watering hole frequented by Bonnie Parker, Clyde Barrow, and other notables. An outspoken teetotaler, O'Daniel forbade the band members to make personal appearances in honky-tonks. The Doughboys began to chafe at O'Daniel's straitlaced, tight-fisted control. Lead singer Milton Brown quit the Doughboys first and formed his own band, the Musical Brownies. Wills was more reluctant to give up his steady gig. After all, O'Daniel had given his father, Jim Wills, a job on the O'Daniel ranch in Aledo, Texas. But O'Daniel treated Jim Wills so badly that at one point Old Man Wills warned his son, "I'm gonna kill that son of a bitch W. Lee O'Daniel."[14] A short time later Jim Wills tried just that, and chased O'Daniel off his own property, threatening him with a three-foot-long piece of oak from a harness. O'Daniel had several dust-ups with Wills the younger, most of them after the fiddle player had been indulging his taste for alcohol. Wills's drinking caused him to miss several performances and even wreck a Light Crust vehicle.

Finally, in August 1933, Bob Wills quit the Doughboys. He formed his own band and moved to Waco, where his band performed as "The Texas Playboys." O'Daniel filed a lawsuit that sought to bar Wills from using the words "Formerly the Light Crust Doughboys" in his advertising. He also claimed $10,000 in damages to Light Crust Flour, arising from Wills's alleged practice of "presenting promiscuous programs" at dances. After more than two years, and after Wills had moved to Oklahoma to get away from his influential and vindictive former boss, the courts threw out O'Daniel's case. When Wills later heard that O'Daniel had instructed the Light Crust Doughboys to punctuate their tunes with a Wills-type yell, he joked, "O'Daniel sued me for stealing a name. Now I'm going to sue him for stealing my holler."[15]

Even after Wills's departure, the popularity of the reformed and renamed Doughboys continued to grow. While the strains of fiddle tunes, western swing, and familiar hymns pleased audiences as much as ever, it was the silver-tongued Pappy who kept Texans glued to the radio. His deep melodic voice was modulated perfectly for the tinny radio speakers of the day, and his homages to motherhood, honesty, and good Christian living pulled at the heartstrings of his audience. He urged erring husbands to correct their ways, called for schoolchildren to be thrifty, and promoted adoption and traffic safety. He was a Texas Babbitt, a good Christian businessman with a sense of humor. One chronicler described his radio persona as "Eddie Guest and Will Rogers and Dale Carnegie and Bing Crosby rolled into one." O'Daniel talked "like a big brother, a pal, a guide, a friend," blending homespun religiosity with humor and good common sense.

Poems and songs seemed to flow effortlessly from the tip of O'Daniel's flour-dusted pen. Listeners hummed along to Texas-proud melodies like "Sons of the Alamo," "The Lay of the Lonely Longhorn," and "Beautiful Texas," as well as celebrations of family values, including "The Boy Who Never Grew Too Old to Comb His Mother's Hair." O'Daniel never learned to write music. He created his musical compositions by writing down lyrics, then whistling the melodies for his band members to pick up.

His radio style was so unorthodox for the times that it made Harold Hough, the manager of WBAP, nervous. Hough carefully blue-penciled each of O'Daniel's scripts, both as a service to his client and as protection for the radio station against controversial programming. "Many times the station refused to allow O'Daniel to read stuff he had written," Hough later recalled. "We couldn't see, for instance, how his telling little boys to walk on the right side of the street and pointers like that could possibly have anything to do with flour selling!"[16] More often than not, Hough was wrong, and O'Daniel's appeals to public service continued to bolster the sale of Light Crust Flour.

The Light Crust Doughboys had such a strong regional reputation that technicians from the American Record Company (ARC) Victor Records invited the band to record a few tunes at the Jefferson Hotel in Dallas on February 9, 1932. The Doughboys were in good company. During the same trip, ARC recorded Jimmie Rodgers, the Yodelling Brakeman, one of the first country music superstars, and Jimmie Davis, creator of the mega-hit "You Are My Sunshine." O'Daniel and his musicians continued to make popular records through the 1930s. Their November 11, 1936, session was just one day before bluesman Robert Johnson attended an ARC session in San Antonio and recorded "Sweet Home Chicago," "Cross Road Blues," and other roots-music classics.

In 1935, O'Daniel departed from Burrus Mills and the Light Crust Doughboys. Some say that O'Daniel decided to leave on his own. Others told a different story. According to the late Light Crust Doughboy veteran Marvin "Smokey" Montgomery,

> Pappy had been taking the band out to play at theaters, getting fifteen dollars for the appearance, and keeping the money for himself. Pappy also had a deal. For every sack of flour he sold, he made so much. When the Doughboys got going, Pappy was making more money than Jack Burrus. Pappy was also using workers from the mill to go down to his farm in Aledo to build barns and do different kinds of work on Burrus Mill time. So, unbeknownst to Pappy, Jack Burrus hires Eddie Dunn to go over and take his place. Jack goes over to his office and waits for him, and when he comes in: "You're fired, Pappy. Get your stuff and go." And he did.[17]

For whatever reason, O'Daniel founded his own company, the W. Lee O'Daniel Company. He bought flour from a milling plant in Wichita Falls and started selling it under his own brand name, Hillbilly Flour. He formed a new band, the Hillbilly Boys, with his own sons, Pat and Mike, on banjo and fiddle. To avoid a recurrence of the Bob Wills experience, he kept his performers anonymous, referring to them by nickname. Pat was Patty-boy. Mike was Mickey Wickey. Carroll Hubbard, who was a teenager when he joined the Hillbilly Boys and actually lived with the O'Daniel

family to help his sons with their musicianship, played fiddle under the stage name "Little Caesar the Fiddle Teaser."[18]

O'Daniel pulled out all the stops to market Hillbilly Flour, using all kinds of marketing gimmicks. His flour sacks were brightly colored with cutouts of his band members on the back, for moms to sew up as dolls for their kids. One of Pappy's immortal verses appeared on the sack beneath an image of a colorful goat:

Pappy O'Daniel and the Hillbilly Boys, 1938. (Courtesy: Fort Worth Star-Telegram Photograph Collection, Special Collections Division, The University of Texas at Arlington Libraries)

> HILLBILLY Music "on the air"
> HILLBILLY Flour everywhere;
> It tickles your feet—it tickles your tongue,
> Wherever you go, Its Praises are sung.

Emblazoned beneath the poem were the words "SATISFACTION GUARANTEED."

Produced in red, yellow, and blue with band-member doll cutouts on the back, Hillbilly Flour sacks were almost as valuable as the flour they contained. (Courtesy: Border Radio Research Institute)

By 1937 the biscuit baron was worth well over $500,000. Thousands of ears across the Southwest perked up when they heard the theme song to the tune of "I Like Mountain Music":

> I like bread and biscuits,
> Big white fluffy biscuits—
> Hillbilly Flour makes 'em grand.
> So while we sing and play
> And try to make folks happy,
> We hope you'll say,
> "Please pass the biscuits, Pappy."

The sophisticated Ohio-born businessman became known as "Please Pass the Biscuits, Pappy" or just plain "Pappy" O'Daniel. He dabbled in real estate and expanded his entertainment horizons by broadcasting from the super-powerful and quasi-legal border radio stations located just south of the Texas-Mexico border. For all his homespun airs and down-home demeanor, the radio star was one of the kingpins of Fort Worth. He wrote most of his copy himself, but he also relied on the advice of Dallas public relations man Phil Fox to help shape his down-home image. He was a tough, successful businessman who was close to some of the richest and most conservative men in the state. O'Daniel's associates included Fort Worth oilman Jesse McKee and insurance magnate Carr P. Collins, a Republican who got involved in the radio business as a marketing operation for his mineral water products, Crazy Water and Crazy Water Crystals.[19]

In the spring of 1938 O'Daniel and his cronies discussed a marketing idea that was as simple as it was revolutionary. Should Pappy enter the 1938 Texas Democratic primary for the governor of the Lone Star State?

At that time, Texas was a one-party state, securely controlled by the Democratic Party. No Republican had served as governor of Texas since 1873, the last year of the Reconstruction administration under Republican governor Edmund J. Davis. With the adoption of the poll tax in 1902, Texas Democrats tightened their grip over the electoral system by effectively disenfranchising many poor white, black, and Hispanic voters. The Terrell Election Laws of 1905 instituted a direct primary system for all statewide candidates. In 1938 the Democratic Party controlled the primary system; winning the Democratic nomination for state office meant winning the office itself.

Pappy was intrigued by the idea of a combination vote-getting/flour-selling campaign. Selling politicians was a lot like selling flour. They were both commodity-type endeavors in which competing products were basically the same thing. The secret to success was in marketing. Intrigued though he was, Pappy was also hesitant. He was a Kansas-bred political novice who had always voted Republican but had not even paid the Texas poll tax. Still, as a hard-driving salesman, he had a gut feeling that running for office would be a great way to sell flour.

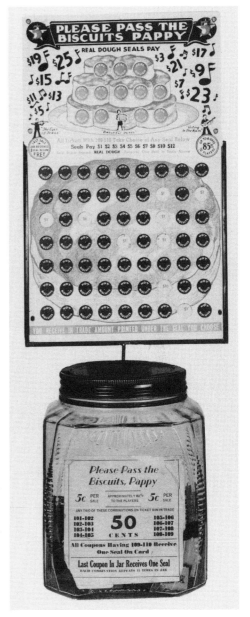

O'Daniel created this point-of-purchase lottery system to help boost sales of Hillbilly Flour. (Courtesy: Texas State Library and Archives Commission, #1983/112-H-95)

On Palm Sunday, 1938, Pappy's fans in radio land heard the familiar greeting "How do you do, ladies and gentlemen, and hello there, boys and girls. This is W. Lee O'Daniel speaking." He spoke warmly, soothingly into the microphone. He told his listeners that a blind man had sent him a letter, saying that he was tired of politics as usual in the state of Texas. The man was looking for a gubernatorial candidate to support in the upcoming Democratic primary, someone who was trustworthy, honest, and a good Christian. The only candidate the listener could think of was Pappy O'Daniel.

The listener begged Pappy to enter the race. Pappy obligingly passed the request on to his radio audience, asking them if he should indeed run for the state's highest office. The audience responded with a flood of mail that dazed even the celebrated master of radio flour power. Pappy reported that 54,499 people wrote in asking him to run for governor. Only four listeners advised against his candidacy.[20]

On Sunday morning, May 1, 1938, O'Daniel announced on a special radio broadcast that he would seek the Democratic nomination for governor of Texas. Speaking to his friends in radio land, O'Daniel declared that his campaign platform was the Ten Commandments and his campaign theme, "Pass the Biscuits, Pappy." His campaign motto was the Golden Rule. He further declared his support for state pensions—$30 per month for every Texan over sixty-five years of age. Pensions were the hot-button political issue of the day. The legislature had added pensions to the Texas constitution in 1935 but had not approved a plan to fund them. When pressed for more details about his campaign, Pappy announced his campaign slogan, "Less Johnson Grass and Politicians, More Smokestacks and Businessmen."[21]

In the first week of June 1938, only six weeks before the Democratic primary election, Pappy launched one of the most remarkable campaigns in American political history. Accompanied by his wife Merle, his daughter Molly, and his sons Pat and Mike and the rest of the Hillbilly Boys, the candidate covered more than 20,000 miles in the Hillbilly Flour promotional bus. Close to 25,000 people gathered to see Pappy in Waco, and 26,000 Hillbilly fans crammed into Miller Memorial Theater in Houston to listen to the flour-selling candidate. It was the biggest political gathering in Texas up to that time.

The response in smaller towns was even more dramatic. When bus trouble delayed the O'Daniel caravan, some 3,000 people waited more than three hours to see Pappy finally arrive in Colorado City, Texas. When the Hillbilly bus tried to pass through Wharton on the way to a rally in Rosenberg, Whartonites blocked the road and demanded that Pappy present the political show they'd heard so much about.

W. LEE O'DANIEL

The "Common Citizen's" Candidate For

GOVERNOR

State Headquarters --- Fort Worth

If and when I am elected Governor of Texas I shall honestly and faithfully perform the duties of that office with fairness to all and special favors to none.

(over)

"Beautiful Texas"

Composed by

W. Lee O'Daniel

1.

You have all read the beautiful stories
Of the countries far over the sea,
From whence came our ancestors
To establish this land of the free.
There are some folks who still like to travel
To see what they have over there,
But when they go look, it's not like the book,
And they find there is none to compare.

CHORUS

(Oh) Beautiful, beautiful Texas,
Where the beautiful bluebonnets grow,
We're proud of our forefathers
Who fought at the Alamo.
You can live on the plains or the mountain
Or down where the sea breezes blow,
And you're still in beautiful Texas,
The most beautiful State that we know.

2.

You can travel on beautiful highways
By the city, the village, and farm,
Or sail up above on the skyways,
And the beauty below you will charm;
White cotton, green forests, blue rivers,
Golden wheat fields, and fruit trees that bear;
You can look 'til doomsday, and then you will say
That Texas has beauty to spare.

3.

In this song about beautiful Texas,
There's one thing we just have to say
About six million people,
Who are proud they're here to stay.
It's great to be healthy and happy,
And that seems to be our good fate,
So let us all smile—for life is worth while
When we live in this beautiful State.

W. LEE O'DANIEL.

OUR SLOGAN

*Less Johnson Grass and Politicians,
More Smokestacks and Business Men*

(over)

In Wharton, Rosenberg, Colorado City, San Antonio, and other towns, the Hill-billy Boys hit the stage and led off with a fiery version of O'Daniel's swinging ode to Depression optimism, "My Million Dollar Smile." Patty-boy, Mickey Wickey, and the rest of the band followed up with a few more popular tunes, like the hit song first recorded by Patsy Montana in 1935, "I Want to Be a Cowboy's Sweetheart." As the crowd warmed to the music, their anticipation began to build.

Finally, the stocky five-foot, ten-inch O'Daniel appeared onstage, his hair carefully slicked back. His round, clean-shaven face broke into a dimpled grin. "Hello,

Attendees at O'Daniel political rallies could sing along with the candidate by following the words to "Beautiful Texas" on the back of this campaign card. (Courtesy: Texas State Library and Archives Commission, #1995/18-1-1, #1995/18-1-2)

E O'DANIEL for GOVERN

Pappy and the Hillbilly Boys on top of their promotional bus at a San Antonio campaign stop during his first race for governor, June 29, 1938. O'Daniel is at the microphone. To his right, holding a fiddle, is his son Mike; to his left is his son Pat, with a banjo. (Courtesy: The Institute of Texan Cultures at UTSA No. L-1897-D, The San Antonio Light Collection)

friends," he said. "This is W. Lee O'Daniel, the next governor of Texas." Before the cheers died down, Pappy led the band in singing his most popular song, "Beautiful Texas."

Between slices of easily digestible political rhetoric, well-known songs, and old-time religion, Pappy gleefully plugged Hillbilly Flour. He claimed openly that he entered the governor's race for one reason and one reason only—to sell more flour. Far from being offended, audiences appreciated his animated spontaneity. "Folks," O'Daniel announced from the campaign platform, "heretofore I've always worked for an honest living, but—look at me now!"[22] And whenever questions from the audience got too pointed, O'Daniel would simply cue the band. "All right, boys, give 'em a tune, just like you did when we were selling Hillbilly Flour."[23]

If, as H. L. Mencken observed, American politics is a "carnival of buncombe," then Pappy O'Daniel was one of its greatest carnies. Beautiful Texas, beautiful faces, million-dollar smiles—Pappy and his Hillbillies were rays of performance sunshine that filled Depression-era Texas. The O'Daniel political show provided a means of escape from the worries of the Depression. Dust bowl conditions and economic stagnation had forced thousands of Texans to leave their rural homes and migrate to urban areas looking for work. A steady job with a big company—that was beautiful. Industrialization was beautiful. The security of an old-age pension was beautiful. Bringing good business methods to the state capital in Austin, where the treasury was running a record deficit of $19 million—that was beautiful. Not only Pappy's songs but also the sound of his poetry and Bible quotations were music to the ears of beleaguered Texans. It was just too much fun. And the people of Texas loved him for it.

At the close of each rally, the candidate took up a collection, passing around small wooden barrels emblazoned with the slogan "Flour Not Pork." It was another political breakthrough for O'Daniel, a fundraising gimmick that enabled his audiences to buy into his campaign for a dime and to thumb their noses at the candidates Pappy derided as "professional politicians." "Who put this twenty dollar bill into the barrel?" O'Daniel asked from onstage, holding out a twenty as if it were a soiled rag. Finally, a sheepish supporter raised his hand. "This is the campaign for the common citizen," O'Daniel declared. "Twenty dollars is too much—one dollar is just enough." And he promptly gave the overzealous donor $19 in change.

At first, newspapermen scoffed at the O'Daniel campaign. But after they witnessed the size and enthusiasm of the enormous crowds that flocked to hear O'Daniel, they had to admit that there was a whole lot of rise in Pappy's political dough. After all, this sort of thing had happened before. Mirabeau Buonaparte Lamar, the second president of the Republic of Texas, was also a poet. Master showman P. T. Barnum served in the Connecticut Legislature in the 1860s and 1870s. In 1930, Dr. John R. Brinkley ran as a write-in candidate for governor of Kansas. A well-known broadcaster who owned the powerful station KFKB (Kansas First, Kansas Best), Brinkley had made a fortune by perfecting the "goat gland proposition," a unique cure for sexual dysfunction that involved the transplantation of goat gonads into the privates of ailing men. Under the slogan "Let's Pasture the Goats on the Statehouse Lawn," Brinkley ran a vigorous, though unsuccessful, campaign, appearing on stage with cowboy singer Roy Faulkner and a preacher who introduced the sunflower-sporting Brinkley as the "modern Moses." Texas political observers even used the term "glandular technique" to describe any campaign built on oversimplified, ever-popular political bromides.[24]

In 1932, Louisiana governor Huey Long appeared on the campaign trail in Arkansas with a caravan of sound trucks described as "a circus hitched to a tornado." The Kingfish turned defeat into victory for U.S. Senate candidate Hattie Caraway. In the same year that Pappy was running for governor in Texas, former South Dakota governor Tom Berry campaigned for a seat in the U.S. Senate with a brass band and a group of Indians in full regalia.[25] Also in 1938, "Singing Cowboy" Glenn H. Taylor, running for the Idaho seat in the U.S. Senate, hit the campaign trail with the Glen- dora Players, a hillbilly group that featured his wife, Dora, and his son Arod. Glenn lost his first and second race for Senate but finally won in 1944, wearing an attractive toupee of his own design.[26]

On July 23, 1938, the day of the primary election, WBAP's Harold Hough, nicknamed the Hired Hand, visited the O'Daniel home, microphone in hand, and talked with the leading contender. Pappy ended the broadcast with one of his acute observations: "This certainly shows the wonderful power of radio in our social, economic, and business life. I mustn't forget business, because I'm still selling Hillbilly Flour, you know, and I've got to get a plug in here. If I should be elected governor, and my family is privileged to live in your mansion, remember that the latch string is always out. Bring your dinners and feed for your horses and spend the day."[27]

Pappy could afford to be cocky. He was already a winner. Sales of Hillbilly Flour doubled during the campaign. As Pappy put it, "A store in Beeville wants two hundred and ten barrels. They say they'll have 'em sold before they get there. . . . I can't

O'Daniel, surrounded by his wife and children, holds a stack of telegrams from supporters as they listen to election returns on the family radio, July 23, 1938. (Courtesy: Fort Worth Star-Telegram Photograph Collection, Special Collections Division, The University of Texas at Arlington Libraries)

begin to tell you how many carloads I've sold this morning. Boy, . . . is business good."[28] Later that year, Pappy attended a rally for the Fort Worth Salesman's Crusade at the Texas Christian University stadium and received a loving cup inscribed with the well-deserved message, "To W. Lee O'Daniel, Texas' No. 1 Salesman of 1938."[29]

While the election results didn't surprise O'Daniel, they stunned his major opponents. Colonel Ernest O. Thompson of Amarillo and William McCraw of Dallas, prominent conservative attorneys, were both convinced that they would defeat O'Daniel in a runoff. To their horror, Pappy won the primary with 50.7 percent of the vote, a simple majority which guaranteed him the Democratic nomination for governor with no runoff.

An estimated 250,000 people cheered Pappy's cavalcade as he drove from Fort Worth to the capital city of Austin for his inauguration on January 17, 1939. On several occasions, schoolchildren ran out into the road, blocking traffic and forcing O'Daniel to say a few words to his supporters. The inauguration ceremony, described by the press as "the greatest fanfare and show of pomp ever witnessed in the state," attracted a crowd of 100,000. The University of Texas Memorial Stadium filled with 60,000 people, including a busload of Confederate veterans, who came to hear the Texas A&M College band, the UT band, and the Hillbilly Boys. Wearing a suit made out of Texas wool woven at Texas Technological College in Lubbock, O'Daniel took the oath of office with his hand on a 133-year-old Bible and became the thirty-third governor of the state, the first radio star to live in the Governor's Mansion.

Pappy himself was confident of his ability to avoid the pitfalls of the professional politicians. One reporter asked him, "You've done a good job of selling, but how are you going to deliver the goods if the machine gets after you?" O'Daniel responded, "I've got my own machine. This little microphone."

On Sunday, January 22, 1939, O'Daniel made a historic step into the aether, becoming only the second governor to broadcast from the Governor's Mansion and the first to broadcast a regular entertainment program. The Hillbilly Boys set themselves up in the Mansion's high-ceilinged, gold-walled drawing room and tuned their instruments, plucking guitars and fiddles while they waited for airtime. Then, as the stately visages of Richard Coke, Michael B. Menard, and others looked on from the walls of the eighty-six-year-old room, the prince of biscuits appeared. Smiling, he greeted the large audience with "Good morning, folks" and took his place behind a battery of microphones. At exactly 8:30 a Hillbilly Boy started playing, and the strains of "Home Sweet Home" floated through the chamber and over the airwaves of the state on the Texas Quality Network.

Pappy raised his rich voice above the sweet music: "Good morning, ladies and gentlemen, and hello there, boys and girls. This is Governor W. Lee O'Daniel speaking. . . . We are in the front room of the Governor's Mansion—and what a room—it has a ceiling so high the boys could fly a kite in it. . . . Be it ever so humble, there's no place like home." He spoke the familiar words in perfect cadence with the music, as he had for so many years in support of Light Crust and Hillbilly flour, while the band played on. Nearby, the O'Daniels' twelve-year-old canary, Jerry, and their goldfish listened to the music.[30] Outside, an angora goat, an admirer's gift, neatly clipped the lawn of the Governor's Mansion.

More than any other governor, Governor Pappy made the people of Texas feel as though the Governor's Mansion was their home.

Even before he took the oath of office, the state's biggest vote-getter had proved that he was a businessman and a promoter, not a politician. During the Democratic

Newly inaugurated governor Wilbert Lee O'Daniel (left) shakes hands with outgoing governor James V. Allred as O'Daniel's daughter, Molly, and 60,000 spectators watch the ceremony at Memorial Stadium on the campus of the University of Texas at Austin, January 17, 1939. (Courtesy: The Institute of Texan Cultures at UTSA No. L-2013-U, The San Antonio Light Collection)

During Governor O'Daniel's term in office, this goat kept the lawn of the Governor's Mansion well trimmed. (Courtesy: Texas State Library and Archives Commission)

convention in the summer of 1938, O'Daniel announced his choices for candidates in the primary runoff to his radio audience, an unprecedented step that no gubernatorial candidate had ever made. Many of Pappy's supporters were shocked. "How could you endorse these professional politicians?" they asked. O'Daniel was booed off the stage at the Democratic Convention in Galveston before he had a chance to explain his proposal for funding old-age pensions. One former supporter from Dallas wrote, "A friend of mine bet me a mule that day after you were nominated that you would make a fool of yourself before you were inaugurated. I am delivering him his mule."[31]

Once in office, Pappy's political performance did not improve. One of his first jobs was to appoint important state officials to implement his programs. Pappy had more trouble with the appointment process than any other governor in Texas history. He did manage to appoint Orville Burlington, a lifelong militant Republican from Wichita Falls, as a regent of the University of Texas. Burlington's appointment, and the appointment of other conservative regents, eventually led to a clampdown on academic freedom at the University, the removal of University president Homer Price Rainey, and a nine-year censorship of the University by the American Association of University Professors.[32]

Governor O'Daniel tried to establish a council of business advisors to help him run the government on a businesslike basis. The council met only once, behind closed doors at the Hotel Texas in Fort Worth. When asked about his pension plan while attending a show in a Fort Worth nightclub, Pappy pointed to a juggler and said, "What that fellow's doing looks impossible, but he's doing it." He got nowhere with his "transaction tax" plan to fund old-age pensions and made enemies of many state legislators, who did not like being called "scheming professional politicians." A loner by nature, the governor became even lonelier as the legislative session progressed. Walking from the Governor's Mansion to the Capitol, he studiously avoided the glances of legislators. One reporter described him as "the loneliest man I ever saw."[33] As Pappy put it, "Seems like that every time I stick my head in an office in Austin to see how they're spending your money, they slam the door in my face."

A master of the media, Pappy could not get along with the press. On February

After O'Daniel's victory in the 1938 gubernatorial election, Son Sheffield (seated) collected on a pre-campaign bet and rode in a wheelbarrow through the streets of Marshall, Texas, followed by a crowd of a thousand O'Daniel rooters singing "Beautiful Texas." (Courtesy: Texas State Library and Archives Commission #2001/138-56-1)

27, 1938, he announced that "the regular Tuesday press conferences will be abandoned," reasoning that news didn't always break on Tuesdays. While he dodged the press, he practiced with his band twice every week for his regular Sunday broadcast from the Governor's Mansion, and he placed his musicians on the state payroll. Leon Huff, for example, who performed as Leon the Texas Songbird, took a job as a clerk in the motor pool for the Texas adjutant general. Fiddle player Cliff Bruner also worked for the adjutant general, as did musician Jim Boyd, who was appointed a colonel in the Texas National Guard and given free housing at Camp Mabry in Austin, only to have it taken away when he quit the governor's band.[34]

The Forty-sixth Legislature ended in the late spring of 1939 without a resolution to the pension crisis. According to press reports, out of 1,642 bills offered, the legislature passed 650, which included no "outstanding" legislation.[35] Despite the weak legislative batting average, Governor Pappy remained immensely popular. From the Governor's Mansion, O'Daniel distributed printed copies of his songs and poems to the good people of Texas. A copy of one poem, "I Love to Hear a Churchbell," was marked at the bottom with the slogan "Use Hillbilly Flour." And he continued to broadcast every Sunday over the radio from the Governor's Mansion.

Pappy's use of free radio time began to cause concern among some of the state's leading media managers. The Federal Communications Commission and officials at the National Association of Broadcasters were extremely leery about using public airwaves for political commentary. In the early 1930s, the CBS radio network aired the radio sermons of Father Charles Coughlin of the Little Flower Church in Royal Oak, Michigan. Instead of confining his comments to religious questions, the crusading priest attacked the gold standard, prohibition, and "machine competition," which he described as "modern industrial slavery." As Coughlin's tirades increased in ferocity, CBS allowed his contract to expire and established a network policy against selling airtime to religious groups, a policy quickly adopted by the other leading radio network, NBC.

In part to protect themselves against radical commentators, the federal regulators and network officials pressured the broadcasting industry to provide equal time for opposing views on any particular issue. Eventually codified, the "fairness doctrine," as it was called, restricted much political commentary from the airwaves until it was abandoned by the FCC in the late 1980s, allowing for the emergence of unanswered political commentary by the talk-radio superstars of today.

Harold Hough and the management of WBAP in Fort Worth decided that

O'Daniel was using his airtime to further his political career, not to inform the citizens of Texas. After O'Daniel's October 15, 1938, broadcast, Hough requested advance copies of all future O'Daniel broadcast scripts. Though advertiser O'Daniel had willingly allowed Hough to review his radio scripts, Governor O'Daniel was outraged by the request and refused to cooperate. WBAP was equally adamant and pulled the governor off the air.

O'Daniel's listening audience in the Fort Worth area was shocked by his disappearance from WBAP. "I was disappointed to tears Sunday morning when you didn't come on at 8:30 o'clock," wrote one woman. "Congratulations! More power to you!" wrote another O'Daniel fan. "We are proud that you refused to submit a transcript of your broadcast to be blue-penciled by the controllers of the radio."

The governor himself was equally outspoken and addressed the issue in his October 29, 1938, radio address. "Now they have set up this censorship of your governor," he began, "and refused to carry my program because I did not let them censor what I had to say. You will remember several months ago that I told you on the radio that I had been informed there was a movement afoot by the professional politicians to have me cut off the air." Some stations followed WBAP's lead and canceled O'Daniel's programs, but most small stations overlooked the matter entirely. They could not afford to lose as popular a program as the Governor Pappy show.

O'Daniel's frustration with the press and the legislature drove him to the border. Technicians at the University of Texas in Austin made electrical transcriptions of Pappy's programs and shipped them to XEAW, the 100,000-watt station located in Reynosa, Mexico, across the border from McAllen, Texas. His speeches were broadcast twice on Sundays, along with advertisements for Hillbilly Flour. Pappy felt that the border radio outlet was so important that he obtained part ownership of a station for himself, partnering with his campaign manager, Carr P. Collins. Opponents like state senator Jerry Sadler struck out against O'Daniel's blasts from the border, suggesting that O'Daniel change his famous slogan from "Pass the Biscuits, Pappy" to "Pass the Tamales, Pappy." Even the *New York Times* took note of Pappy's break for the border in a story headlined "Waves that Cross the Rio Grande."[36]

Pappy's second gubernatorial campaign was not as easy as his first. Leon Huff quit the band and went to work for the opposition, singing for state senator Jerry Sadler's campaign band, Sadler's Cowboy Stringsters.[37] O'Daniel blamed the flight of the Texas Songbird on "the gang of professional politicians," although Huff eventually told the press, "I quit because my conscience would not let me work for a man who broke his pledge and made no consideration for anyone but himself." Another entertainer was much more blunt in his assessment of Pappy, describing the flour-peddling politician as "a horse's ass of the first water."

On the gubernatorial campaign trail for the second time in 1940, O'Daniel lost much of his humor. He railed against "the poison pen editors of the big newspapers, the lesser lights of cartoonists, 'stinking out loud' columnists, and 'give-me-an-offer' story writers." Those who opposed his plan for funding pensions in the legislature were "a little bunch of pin-headed legislators so pig-headed as to keep the sovereign voters from voting on anything." He ended his campaign in Abilene, leading the band in a song of his creation, "There Ain't Gonna Be No Runoff."

Despite the change in the tone of his rhetoric, Pappy's popularity had been steadily on the rise since the close of the forty-sixth legislative session in 1939. Pollsters attributed the phenomenon to "the paucity of political activity that might have engendered opposition." O'Daniel was much better at attending functions and issuing proclamations for Yam Week, Bottled Soft Drink Week, and Black-eyed Pea Day than he was at fighting the hard battles of the legislature. On Election Day he retained the support of the rural population and the older people who still believed that he was "a good Christian man." As one supporter put it, "He's a good man. It ain't his fault he didn't do nothing." O'Daniel got 53.7 percent of the votes cast for governor in the biggest turnout recorded up to that time in a gubernatorial election, some 100,000 votes more than the combined votes of his six opponents.

After his stunning re-election, Governor Pappy took off on a tour of the state with the intention of visiting every state legislator he could. He declared that he wanted no meetings or speeches or banquets on the trip, but wanted to drive up to the homes of the legislators and "visit with them and see how they live."[38]

With a sleeping car of his own design, modified by the state garage, and a staff photographer from the Department of Public Safety, Governor O'Daniel logged, by his estimation, more than 7,500 miles in just over five weeks from September through October 1940, and visited 90 percent of the state's legislators. Merle, the first lady of Texas, accompanied him on the entire grueling trip. Photographs taken during this journey make up the bulk of this book, a stunning visual record of Texas and its political leaders at the dawn of World War II.

While these visual images are rich, written records providing information on the activities and backgrounds of the legislators is unfortunately poor. No guide publicly or privately produced provides detailed biographical information on individual legislators. Until taping of the legislative proceedings commenced in 1973, no records were kept of legislative floor debates or committee meetings. There was little press coverage of goings-on in the legislature. Editors and reporters felt that readers were not particularly interested in what one reporter described as "a circus of ordinary follies."[39]

Being a member of the Texas legislature wasn't, and still isn't, a glamour job. The legislature met, and still meets, in Austin every two years for a 120-day session, often followed by a number of special sessions. The brief legislative window was specified by the Texas Constitution of 1876, a document drafted by a post-Reconstruction Texas that had little use for politicians.

Despite O'Daniel's protestations, there weren't many professional politicians in Texas, because so few could afford to be. Legislators earned just $10 per day for the first 120 days of the legislative session and $5 per day for each additional day. This was in addition to a travel allowance to and from Austin of ten cents a mile. Many legislators could afford to serve only because a herd of lobbyists helped defray their costs and ease their pains by offering "three B's"—bourbon, beef, and blondes.[40]

The Texas Constitution allows for 31 senators and 150 representatives. Due to resignations and death, 33 senators and 157 representatives served in the Forty-seventh Legislature, including 93 new representatives and 10 new senators, an unusually large freshman class. The socioeconomic makeup of the Forty-seventh Legislature was fairly typical. It included 19 farmers/ranchers who could take time off in the early part of the year, a few businessmen, some older statesman retired from the world of business, 18 teachers, 5 law students, a drugstore clerk, an undertaker, a minister, a garage man, a common laborer, and 57 lawyers, whose partners could afford to carry them and whose practices benefited from contacts made with state bureaucrats. Two women served in the legislature, both in the House of Representatives: Miss Rae Files, a teacher, and Mrs. Neveille H. Colson, a law student.[41]

After finishing his tour of the state, Pappy invited everyone to come to a free inauguration barbecue on the grounds of the Governor's Mansion. Roughly 20,000 Texans took the governor up on his invitation, an event that was dutifully recorded for posterity in photographs and motion pictures taken by the Texas Department of Public Safety (see pp. 161–163). After the barbecue, the Forty-seventh Legislature got down to business on January 14, 1941. Once again, O'Daniel failed miserably in gaining legislative approval for most of his political appointments. His appointments to the Texas Liquor Control Board were particularly inappropriate. They included a prohibitionist Methodist minister, the head of United Texas Drys, and the president of the Women's Christian Temperance Union.

Frustrated, O'Daniel applied the "glandular technique" to his radio addresses. He warned his listeners that "disease germs are the greatest sabotage agents loose in Texas today" and urged his fellow Texans to "keep our bodies clean and strong and our minds pure and healthy." In addition to his stand against destructive micro-organisms, he began a campaign against evil macro-organisms, those scheming fifth columnists who participated in un-American activities. He wired President Roosevelt with the news that he had confidential information concerning the activities of fifth columnists in Texas and asked his listening audience to inform his office of any un-American activity they might observe. Hundreds of faux G-men, including a "park bench warmer," flooded the governor's office with dubious leads.

While O'Daniel was busy ferreting out fifth columnists, the Texas Legislature managed to pass a tax bill to pay for pensions. The governor at first described the bill as "stinking" but eventually supported it and even took credit for it. By that time, O'Daniel's attention was once again drawn to the campaign trail.

On April 9, 1941, U.S. Senator Morris Sheppard, a sixty-five-year-old Texas Democrat and the father of national prohibition, passed away. According to his physician, Sheppard died from overwork as the chairman of the Senate Military Affairs Committee struggling to prepare America for the inevitable world war.

On April 19, Governor O'Daniel announced that a special election would be held June 28 for Sheppard's vacated Senate seat. In the interim, state law required O'Daniel to appoint a "suitable and qualified" candidate to serve in Washington. On April 21, 1941, the 105th anniversary of the Battle of San Jacinto, Pappy addressed a radio audience from the auditorium of the San Jacinto Monument, a 570-foot-tall limestone-faced monument marking the historic battlefield. Over a statewide radio hookup, O'Daniel recalled the victory of the Texians over the Mexican forces and extolled the virtues of the victorious commander in that campaign, General Sam Houston, who became the first president of the independent nation of Texas. Then, O'Daniel announced his appointment for U.S. Senator from Texas—eighty-seven-year-old General Andrew Jackson Houston, the only surviving son of General Sam (see pp. 170–171.)

Texas shook its collective head at O'Daniel's appointment of the aged Republican. Houston was the oldest man ever to become a U.S. senator. It seemed almost cruel to send the octogenarian with dim eyes, unsteady steps, and wasted flesh to work in Washington, D.C., at the outbreak of World War II. "Well, that man probably couldn't tell you whether the sun was up or had gone down," veteran legislator Claude Gilmer recalled. "I mean he was in his dotage."[42] Houston's daughters didn't want their father to make the journey to Washington for health reasons. But Houston answered the call to duty, traveled to the nation's capital, took the oath of office, attended one committee meeting, and passed away a short time later. O'Daniel sent Houston's relatives a telegram of condolence praising the senator's father for his glorious stand at the Alamo, a stand he had never made.

Meanwhile, back in Texas, the race for the U.S. Senate seat quickly turned into a salute to political zaniness, Texas-style. It was the first statewide special election for the sole purpose of selecting only one man for office. Anyone who filed his name on time and paid the $1 filing fee could enter the race. The race quickly took the bizarre show biz flavor of the 2003 special election for California governor. *Time* magazine called the 1940 Texas special election the "biggest carnival in American politics."[43] *Life* magazine ran the headline "27 Candidates Seek Senate Seat in Screwy Texas Race" and printed photos of several of the more theatrical candidates, including tax opponent E. A. Calvin, who campaigned attired in a wooden barrel; the Reverend Sam Morris, known as the Voice of Temperance; W. W. King, who favored the annexation of Canada; and Dr. John R. Brinkley, creator of the "glandular technique."[44]

The strongest candidate was U.S. Representative Lyndon Baines Johnson, whose congressional district represented Austin and the surrounding hill country. Running with the campaign motto "Roosevelt and Unity" and standing on a platform of "Roosevelt, Roosevelt, Roosevelt," Johnson and his well-oiled machine appeared to be bound for victory, until Pappy declared on May 15, 1941, that he would also enter the race for the U.S. Senate. Pappy took to the airwaves, telling his audience about his "old, old friend the President" and his trusted campaign companions, "the Ten Commandments, the Golden Rule, an inbred and inerasable common touch with the common man, and, I hope, your unceasing prayers." Immediately after the announcement, LBJ fell sick for two weeks, smitten with the indigestible realization that he was up against the greatest vote getter in Texas history.

O'Daniel was confident that he would win the campaign handily, but his radio persona had lost most of the humorous warmth that had been so appealing for so many years. O'Daniel compared the politicians in Washington to "stinkweed." He claimed that Roosevelt had surrounded himself with "a group of pussyfooting, pusillanimous politicians who were not fit to run a peanut stand," using the same sort of rhyming rhetoric that Vice President Spiro Agnew would invoke three decades later.

The hobbled governor wanted to be out on the campaign trail, but a stubborn, slow-moving legislature held him in Austin. He couldn't leave town until the legislature adjourned, and the legislature, many of whom supported O'Daniel's opponents, refused to adjourn. Stuck in Austin, O'Daniel sent Molly, Pat, Mike, and the rest of the Hillbilly Boys out on the campaign trail with recordings of his voice. At one rally the recording got stuck. The crowd guffawed as they listened to Governor Pappy declare, "I want to go to Washington to work for the old folks—the old folks—the old folks . . ."

Meanwhile, Johnson bounced out of his sickbed to launch a Pappy-style political road show, featuring an "All-out Patriotic Revue," a minstrel show and lottery which awarded defense bonds and stamps to lucky attendees, a refreshing reversal of the normal cash flow at political events.[45]

Finally freed from his legislative duties, O'Daniel launched his own senatorial campaign on June 18, just ten days before the election. Supporters took movie posters for the brand new film *Mr. Smith Goes to Washington,* crossed out "Mr. Smith," and replaced it with "Mr. O'Daniel."[46] Pappy traveled with the same Capitol-dome sound truck he had used in the 1940 gubernatorial campaign, and he relied on his Hillbilly band to entertain the crowds with their old favorites. But O'Daniel's words had lost their charm. He suggested that Texas form its own army and navy to protect the southern borders and accused Texas newspapers of being "instruments of the devil." He coined the phrase "Communistic labor-leader racketeers" and used it to attack just about everyone. The phrase appeared fourteen times in one speech, sixteen times in another.[47] Pappy's voice filled the airwaves as he broadcast his political pronouncements every day over his border station XEAW and a dozen Texas stations. Johnson gobbled up huge chunks of airtime, appearing on the radio five times a day, making the 1941 race for U.S. Senate one of the first all-out broadcasting media blitz campaigns in the annals of American political history.[48] Johnson appreciated the power of the media to such an extent that he and his family acquired ownership of radio and television stations in Austin, Texas, one of which broadcasts to this day as KLBJ.

With 96 percent of the votes counted, Johnson led O'Daniel by 5,000 votes. The *Dallas News* headline blared, "Only Miracle Can Keep FDR's Anointed Out."[49] But in Texas politics, miracles do happen. Over the next few days, more than a dozen counties came in with "corrected returns," giving the 175,590 to 174,279 victory to O'Daniel by a margin of just 1,311 votes. Pollsters commented that the "amazing change of votes . . . baffles all mathematical laws."[50] Perhaps it baffled other laws as well. In the words of one Johnson strategist, "[O'Daniel] stole more votes than we did, that's all."[51]

Some political observers surmised that the Texas liquor interests had a hand in pushing O'Daniel over the top because they were so anxious to get the teetotaling governor out of the state. Johnson, who suffered the only electoral defeat of his career in the 1941 campaign against O'Daniel, learned an important lesson about the costs and benefits of late returns. Johnson eventually won O'Daniel's Senate seat in an equally questionable election involving late election returns. Out of 988,295 votes cast in the 1948 primary for the Democratic senatorial candidate, Johnson won by just 87 votes, a victory that earned him the nickname "Landslide Lyndon."

Before he left for Washington, Pappy invited the state of Texas to the Governor's Mansion in Austin for one final event, the marriage of his daughter, Molly, to oilman Jack Wrather (see pages 178–179). The wedding was only the third one held in the Governor's Mansion to that time and marked the end of the O'Daniel era in Texas politics.

Once O'Daniel moved to Washington, his political career rapidly declined. He quickly made enemies of his colleagues in the Senate and the members of the national press corps. His legislative ineptitude was described as "so overwhelming as to be embarrassing." Former governor Dan Moody accurately observed, "O'Daniel is as lost in the U.S. Senate as I would be on a circus trapeze."

O'Daniel entered the race for a full Senate term in 1942. He won the Democratic primary, but with less than a majority of the votes. Forced into a runoff election for the first time in his political career, Pappy turned vicious, referring to his opponent, former governor Judge James J. Allred, as "a squirt" and "my little yes man." He labeled Allred's supporters "skunks, buzzards, wolves, thugs, termites, pirates, outlaws, racketeers, and hatchet brigades." In the end, Pappy won the bitter runoff campaign with 51 percent of the vote.

The bitterness and acrimony that marked the 1942 senatorial campaign accompanied O'Daniel for the rest of his political career. He fought with fellow Texas senator Tom Connally and drew the ire of his party by voting with Republicans more than 80 percent of the time. He feuded openly with his old friend, supporter, and business partner Carr P. Collins over the issue of civil rights. Even Pappy's down-home radio poetry took on an unsavory tone: "Yes, friends," he recited over the radio. "Way down south in the land of cotton, when the New Deal's gone but not forgotten, we'll still be segregating, and we'll still be voting straight. Whites and blacks respect each other, but they don't intend to mate . . . This is your United States Senator, W. Lee O'Daniel, speaking from your nation's capital, Washington, D.C., and wishing you, one and all, a pleasant good day."

In 1944, as the world war raged, Pappy joined the Texas Regulars, a group of dissident conservatives who left the Democratic Party in opposition to President Roosevelt's nomination for a fourth term. The Regulars platform called for "Return of states rights, which have been destroyed by the Communist-controlled New Deal." And "Restoration of the supremacy of the white race, which has been destroyed by the Communist-controlled New Deal."[52]

On November 2, Senator O'Daniel traveled to Houston to deliver an anti-Roosevelt speech over a statewide radio hookup. An antagonistic crowd of 3,000 came to the City Auditorium to see what their junior senator had to say. Shortly after O'Daniel appeared at the microphone, a group of 500 rioted, throwing eggs and tomatoes in Pappy's direction and shouting, "We want Roosevelt." Pappy was escorted from the building and later blamed the unpleasantness on "Communistic labor-leader racketeers."

O'Daniel's popularity only fell further over the next few years, and he wisely chose not to run for re-election to the Senate in 1948. He moved back to Texas and founded the W. Lee O'Daniel Life Insurance Company. He briefly reentered politics and ran unsuccessfully for governor in 1956 and 1958 on an anti-Communist pro-segregation platform. Willie Morris, who accompanied the governor briefly, described O'Daniel as "a lonely old man trying to retrieve the past."[53]

At a café in Fort Stockton, O'Daniel walked up to a group of cowboys and stuck out his hand and said, "Hello there, I'm W. Lee O'Daniel and I'm runnin' for Governor." One cowboy replied, "Pappy O'Daniel? I thought he was dead."[54]

On May 12, 1969, Wilbert Lee O'Daniel, the man who had passed so many biscuits and uplifted so many spirits with his hillbilly music and down-home poetry, passed away.

The political career of W. Lee "Please Pass the Biscuits, Pappy" O'Daniel anticipated the modern era of Texas politics, where no Republican's heard a discouraging word and the sky's full of political broadcasting all day. O'Daniel proved the power of the broadcasting media as an electoral tool. Radio was the only truly mass medium in 1938. Politicians long understood radio's power as a communication tool. As early as 1916, radio pioneers broadcast returns on election night. During the 1924 presidential campaign, radio broadcast major speeches, the conventions, and a pre-election-day speech by President Coolidge that went out over a nationwide network to over twenty million listeners.

In 1933, President Franklin Delano Roosevelt effectively began using the inti-

macy of his nationally broadcast "fireside chats" to calm a nation suffering from the worst economic collapse in American history. Later in the decade, the President's son Elliot moved to Texas and purchased Fort Worth radio station KFJZ. In July 1938, Elliot set up the largest network in Texas history, one that included all 31 radio stations in the state, to carry an address by his father from the garden of Elliot's home outside of Fort Worth.[55]

While Roosevelt and other political veterans understood the value of using radio as a communications tool, it was O'Daniel who proved once and for all the vote-getting magnetism of the microphone. According to Seth Shepard McKay, author of the masterful *W. Lee O'Daniel and Texas Politics, 1938–1942*, "He had no political organization of any kind, no campaign manager except Mrs. O'Daniel, no newspaper support in the earlier part of the contest and was totally lacking in political experience. The only possible conclusion is that the O'Daniel victory of 1938 was due to the power of the radio, or perhaps to the skill of O'Daniel in the use of the radio."[56]

While big-time politicians had become mass media personalities, O'Daniel was one of the first mass media personalities to become a big-time politician. The roster of politicians who followed in O'Daniel's electromagnetic wake includes the following: Sonny Bono, who graduated from being Cher's sidekick to a seat in the U.S. House of Representatives; Fred Grandy, who parlayed his role as Gopher on the *Love Boat* TV series into a congressional seat from Iowa; Ben Jones, formerly Cooter in the TV series *Dukes of Hazzard,* who lost his seat in the U.S. House of Representatives to Newt Gingrich; Jesse Ventura, who wrestled his way from the airwaves to the Minnesota governor's mansion; and movie star Ronald Reagan, one of the most beloved American presidents of all time. Reagan began his public career as a radio announcer, and returned to the airwaves as a conservative radio commentator prior to launching his enormously successful 1980 presidential campaign.

More than anyone else, W. Lee "Please Pass the Biscuits, Pappy" O'Daniel resembles Arnold Schwarzenegger, the Republican strong man and political novice who leveraged body building and media stardom into a successful run for the California governor's office in 2003, a run that political commentators described as "crazy." Commenting on the California gubernatorial election, Martin Kaplan, associate dean of the University of Southern California Annenberg School for Communication, observed, "There's no longer any blurry line between show business and politics."[57] W. Lee O'Daniel was the first entertainer to obliterate that line.

O'Daniel's rhetoric was as trailblazing as his manipulation of the media. He took a strong pro-business stance, poked fun at professional politicians, and anchored his politics to the Bible, home, and mother. Like Ross Perot, O'Daniel was a consummate salesman who kept his message simple and knew how to close a deal with each and every voter. In his conservative, pro-business, anti–professional politician rhetoric, O'Daniel was the forefather of Rush Limbaugh, Bill O'Reilly, and the bevy of conservative talk show hosts who wield such a profound effect on today's political discourse. Unlike today's performers, O'Daniel was his own producer, syndicator, and sponsor. O'Daniel never bothered with guests or call-ins. He did all the talking himself, and Texans liked what they heard.

An argument can be made that O'Daniel was actually the first Republican governor of Texas in the post-Reconstruction era. Throughout O'Daniel's political career, Texas was a one-party state, ruled by the Democratic Party. Though many Texas Democrats, including O'Daniel, held more conservative views than many Republicans, they realized that if they jumped to the Republican Party, they had no chance of electoral victory. O'Daniel, well aware of this, had jumped the other way and ran as a Democrat despite his history of voting Republican when he voted at all. Before his first gubernatorial campaign, a Kansas reporter observed that O'Daniel had "never voted any ticket but the Republican. Formerly he lived in Kingman, Kansas, and always voted a Republican ticket. Mr. O'Daniel voted the Republican ticket once in Texas and has never voted the Democratic ticket in Texas or any place else."[58] Alexander Boynton, O'Daniel's Republican opponent in his first gubernatorial election, claimed that O'Daniel was indeed a Republican and therefore ineligible to run on the Democratic ticket.

The photographs collected in the present volume are a powerful evocation of O'Daniel's political glory years. They were years of great depression and great elation, as Texans sought relief from their economic hardship through the colorful personality and homespun philosophy of the most popular entertainer ever to inhabit the Governor's Mansion. Pappy's pro-business stance, combined with his Christian faith, helped crystallize the moral, political, and economic conservatism which has been the predominant sentiment in Texas politics down to the present day.

Just as Joel and Ethan Coen employed a team of professional film makers to portray a fictionalized Pappy in *O Brother, Where Art Thou?* so the photographers from the Texas Department of Public Safety worked hard to capture on film the real Pappy—a grinning, baby-cuddling, turkey-stroking, buffalo-shooting Chief Executive Officer. And from 1938 to 1941, Governor W. Lee "Please Pass the Biscuits, Pappy" O'Daniel encouraged the Lone Star State's visual craftsmen to click away and compile this extraordinary photographic portrait of beautiful, beautiful Texas.

NOTES

1. Seth Shepard McKay, *W. Lee O'Daniel and Texas Politics, 1938–1942* (Lubbock: Texas Technological College Press, 1944), p. 7.

2. George Norris Green, *The Establishment in Texas Politics: The Primitive Years, 1938–1957* (Westport, Conn.: Greenwood Press, 1979), p. 43.

3. Wayne Gard, "Texas Kingfish," *New Republic,* June 23, 1941.

4. McKay, *W. Lee O'Daniel and Texas Politics,* p. 38.

5. Gene Fowler and Bill Crawford, *Border Radio: Quacks, Yodelers, Pitchmen, Psychics, and Other Amazing Broadcasters of the American Airwaves* (Austin: University of Texas Press, 2002), p. 169. All facts and quotes not credited to other sources are from this work, which was co-written by the author.

6. Frank Goodwyn, *Lone-Star Land: Twentieth Century Texas in Perspective* (New York: Alfred A. Knopf, 1955), p. 264.

7. McKay, *W. Lee O'Daniel and Texas Politics,* p. 13.

8. Ibid., p. 10.

9. C. L. Douglas and Francis Miller, *The Life Story of W. Lee O'Daniel* (Dallas: Regional Press, 1938), p. 4. Goodwyn, *Lone-Star Land,* p. 249.

10. Charles R. Townsend, *San Antonio Rose: The Life and Music of Bob Wills* (Urbana and Chicago: University of Illinois Press, 1976), p. 69.

11. Ibid., p. 71.

12. Meacham family papers, University of Texas at Arlington Libraries.

13. Richard Schroeder, *Texas Signs On: The Early Days of Radio and Television* (College Station: Texas A&M University Press, 1998), p. 94.

14. Townsend, *San Antonio Rose,* p. 75.

15. Ibid., p. 82.

16. Douglas and Miller, *Life Story,* p. 103.

17. Schroeder, *Texas Signs On,* p. 100.

18. Jean A. Boyd, *The Jazz of the Southwest: An Oral History of Western Swing* (Austin: University of Texas Press, 1998), p. 49.

19. Green, *The Establishment in Texas Politics,* p. 25.

20. McKay, *W. Lee O'Daniel and Texas Politics,* p. 32.

21. Green, *The Establishment in Texas Politics,* p. 23.

22. Douglas and Miller, *Life Story,* p. 123.

23. Ibid., p. 116.

24. Green, *The Establishment in Texas Politics,* p. 9.

25. McKay, *W. Lee O'Daniel and Texas Politics,* p. 56.

26. Bill Crawford, *Democrats Do the Dumbest Things* (Los Angeles: Renaissance Books, 2000), p. 137.

27. Douglas and Miller, *Life Story,* pp. 147–149.

28. Ibid., 153.

29. *Fort Worth Star-Telegram,* August 12, 1938.

30. Carl R. McQueary, *Dining at the Governor's Mansion* (College Station: Texas A&M University Press, 2003), p. 156.

31. McKay, *W. Lee O'Daniel and Texas Politics,* p. 65.

32. Goodwyn, *Lone-Star Land,* pp. 299–302.

33. Robert A. Caro, *The Path to Power: The Years of Lyndon Johnson, Volume I* (New York, Vintage Books, 1990), p. 703.

34. Boyd, *Jazz of the Southwest,* p. 174.

35. *Dallas Morning News,* January 1, 1941.

36. Sam Robins, "Waves That Cross the Rio Grande," *New York Times,* February 6, 1938.

37. McKay, *W. Lee O'Daniel and Texas Politics,* p. 311.

38. Ibid., p. 343.

39. Willie Morris, *North toward Home* (New York: Vintage Books, 2000), p. 203.

40. Ibid., p. 212.

41. Roster and Standing Committees, Forty-seventh Legislature, The Senate and House of

Representatives of Texas, 1941.

42. Green, *The Establishment in Texas Politics,* p. 34.

43. Caro, *Path to Power,* p. 711.

44. *Life,* June 30, 1941.

45. Caro, *Path to Power,* p. 710.

46. Goodwyn, *Lone-Star Land,* p. 278.

47. Ibid., p. 279.

48. Caro, *Path to Power,* p. 730.

49. Ibid., p. 733.

50. Green, *The Establishment in Texas Politics,* p. 37.

51. Caro, *Path to Power,* p. 740.

52. Green, *The Establishment in Texas Politics,* p. 50.

53. Morris, *North toward Home,* p. 260.

54. Ibid., p. 265.

55. Schroeder, *Texas Signs On,* p. 106.

56. McKay, *W. Lee O'Daniel and Texas Politics,* p. 49.

57. Bernard Weintraub, "Staging Politics as Entertainment," *New York Times,* Sunday, August 10, 2003, Section 4, p. 5.

58. McKay, *W. Lee O'Daniel and Texas Politics,* p. 343.

DPS Photographs,
1939–1941

Soon after his election as governor of Texas in 1938, Pappy O'Daniel observed, "History will record whether or not our administration is good, but surely nobody doubts it will be different. . . . You ain't seen nothin' yet."

One of the main differences between Governor O'Daniel and his predecessors was that Governor O'Daniel was a radio star and the first to broadcast a regular radio program from the Governor's Mansion.

"Hello there boys and girls," he announced to his listeners on October 30, 1939, as this photo was taken. "This is W. Lee O'Daniel speaking . . . I wonder how many of you boys and girls now listening have heard that salutation on the radio before? I have thus greeted you for many years. . . . Now, since the citizens of Texas have elevated me to the highest office in the state, I still have the same interest in your welfare, and as governor, I am glad to give you the same advice and I was mighty proud to issue the Governor's Proclamation of School Safety Week."

Austin, Texas. Governor O'Daniel speaking over the radio from the State Capitol, October 30, 1939. (Courtesy of Chuck Bailey)

Austin, Texas, with Molly O'Daniel in front of the Governor's Mansion, January 22, 1940. (Texas State Library and Archives Commission #1976/8-194)

Built in 1856, the Governor's Mansion in Austin is surrounded by a tall brick wall and intense security. Not so in Governor O'Daniel's time. The governor bragged that during his first year in office, more than 20,000 people visited the Mansion. "We like it," Governor O'Daniel told his radio audience, "and want all of you who now listen no matter where you live, to drop in and visit us—the latch string is always hanging out—Yes, sir, may I repeat—bring your dinner and horse and stay all day . . . in our HOME SWEET HOME."

Here, the governor frolics in the front yard of his home sweet home with his seventeen-year-old daughter, Molly.

"It surely is refreshing to get in front of this friendly old microphone," O'Daniel declared during one of his regular Sunday morning broadcasts from what he called the "front room" of the Governor's Mansion. "It makes me feel that I am seated in your own front room, with two children playing around on the floor and the old folks rocking in the old rocking chair."

Governor O'Daniel combined conservative business values with hillbilly charm as he shared the microphone with James Lewis Kraft, the inventor of processed cheese and a major radio advertiser. The flour-selling governor and his food industry companion stand in front of the Hillbilly Boys, including Governor O'Daniel's sons Mike (holding the fiddle) and Pat (standing to O'Daniel's right).

Austin, Texas, with James Lewis Kraft and the Hill-billy Boys at the Governor's Mansion, March 10, 1940. (Texas State Library and Archives Commission #1976/8-199)

After a reception hosted by Governor O'Daniel for members of the legislative staff, Molly O'Daniel talks with the first family's staff in the kitchen of the Governor's Mansion. The first lady of Texas, Merle O'Daniel, had some reservations about the people who worked in the historic edifice. "It's beautiful, but the servant problem worries me a little bit," she confided to a reporter. "You see, they use prison help—trustees, I think they call them—and it seems the cook was a murderer. Of course, I believe in giving everybody a chance, but supposing I don't like the cooking?"

Austin, Texas, the Governor's Mansion, Molly O'Daniel with the kitchen staff. (Texas State Library and Archives Commission 1976/8-21)

Austin, Texas, the Governor's Mansion, September 8, 1940. (Texas State Library and Archives Commission #1976/198-2)

Even as a boy, Governor O'Daniel claimed "when I grow up and get married I'm going to have two boys and a girl, and call them Pat, Mike, and Molly."

In this family portrait, taken at the Governor's Mansion just before the O'Daniels embarked on a statewide trip to visit all members of the Forty-seventh Legislature in their homes, Merle is seated next to the fifty-year-old governor. Behind, from left to right, stand twenty-one-year-old Pat, twenty-year-old Mike, and seventeen-year-old Molly.

Mrs. O'Daniel admitted that when Pappy insisted on calling their firstborn Pat, "I didn't like that much, but finally agreed, thinking I could change his name later, but the name Pat stuck and so it is today. The name is not Patrick; it's just Pat and there is no middle name or initial." The same was true for Molly and Mike.

Windom, Texas, at the
home of Representative
Choice Moore, fall 1940.
(Texas State Library and
Archives Commission
#1976/8-311)

O'Daniel stands at the microphone

on the porch of the weathered home of Representative Choice Moore, an attorney and farmer from Windom, Texas. Located ten miles east of Bonham in east central Fannin County, Windom reportedly was named for its windblown location. Like many small Texas towns, Windom was hard hit by the Great Depression. Almost the entire population of about 300 appears to have gathered to see the governor. Governor O'Daniel was particularly popular with radio listeners in the small towns of rural Texas. As the mother of an anti-O'Daniel man put it, "Son, I've been having breakfast with Lee O'Daniel on the radio . . . for the past eight years, and I know he's a good man."

"I want to visit these members in their own homes and meet all the members of their families, and just have a good old-fashioned visit," Governor O'Daniel told his radio audience before setting out on his Texas tour. "I simply want to get well acquainted with each and every one of them in a personal manner."

In Trenton, a town of about 490 in extreme southwestern Fannin County, O'Daniel met with Representative John W. Connelly. Like many of his constituents, Representative Connelly was a farmer who was probably involved in the production and shipping of onions, the area's most important crop. While most of the crowd was drawn to the words of O'Daniel, a young boy on the right of the photo (facing page) seems more interested in the cameraman.

Trenton, Texas, Pappy and Merle at the home of Representative John W. Connelly (above) and with Representative John W. Connelly and a member of his family (afacing page), fall 1940. (Texas State Library and Archives Commission #1976/8-316, #1976/8-318)

Wortham, Texas, with Rep-
resentative J. P. Stubbs, fall
1940. (Texas State Library
and Archives Commission
#1976/8-340)

The people of Wortham crowded downtown to hear their governor and his host, Representative J. P. Stubbs, a farmer. The town, located in extreme western Freestone County, had seen better times. In 1924, Wortham boomed with the discovery of the Wortham oilfield. The population exploded from 1,000 to 30,000. By the time of O'Daniel's visit, boom had turned to bust, and the population of 2,000 was struggling with plummeting oil and cotton prices. The governor addressed his audience from a temporary stage built next to a Ford delivery van from the Burleson Funeral Home, located across the street. Always the booster, O'Daniel probably encouraged his audience with the same message he once delivered to his radio audience, "Don't let anybody worry about Texas . . . The rest of the world may be in a mess, but Texas is OK."

Using innovative camera angles, Department of Public Safety Photographer Joe Tisdale captured the thrill of a visit by the governor to Groesbeck, the county seat of Limestone County with a population of about 2,200. Most probably, Governor Pappy chose to pick up the "Howdy Doody" look-a-like from the crowd of excited schoolchildren (below). The pictures seem to be taken at recess or at an impromptu moment. As Governor O'Daniel later told his radio listeners, "We had a wonderful trip . . . greeting the school boys and girls when they gathered in groups, and stopping at schools when we passed by during recess, and saying hello, and in one instance I bummed a ride on a school bus and the little boys and girls sang 'Beautiful Texas' for me as we rode along."

Groesbeck, Texas, with Representative Don Dove and schoolchildren, fall 1940. (Texas State Library and Archives Commission #1976/8-348, #1976/8-356)

Representative Warren Henderson, an attorney, and his family pose on the porch of their home in Marlin, the seat of Falls County. Marlin was best known for its hot mineral springs that drew visitors from across the state and the country. Billing itself as "The Carlsbad of America, the South's Greatest Health Resort Where Life Giving Waters Flow," Marlin hosted the New York Giants baseball spring training camp from 1908 to 1919. Perhaps the young cowgirls holding hands in the photo enjoyed the benefits of Marlin's healing waters.

Marlin, Texas, with Representative Warren Henderson, fall 1940. (Texas State Library and Archives Commission #1976/8-357)

Elgin, Texas, with Repre-
sentative and Mrs. J. O.
Smith, fall 1940. (Texas
State Library and Archives
Commission #1976/8-374)

Located in north Bastrop County, Elgin took pride in its well-known sausage factory and two brick plants, for which it earned the nickname "Brick Capital of the Southwest." As with most Texas towns, Elgin took almost as much pride in its high school band, posing here with the governor and Representative J. O. Smith, a publisher.

Few Texas politicians appreciated the power of music as much as Governor O'Daniel, who wrote dozens of songs besides "Beautiful Texas." "You have heard much lately by some of our would-be-sophisticated stock belittling HILLBILLY music as base and without place in certain high places," the governor once told his radio family. "Well, let them rave on."

On his trip across the state, Governor O'Daniel rarely passed up the opportunity to hold a baby. Here the governor poses with a youngster at the home of twenty-nine-year-old Representative W. T. McDonald, attorney and A&M graduate. When he wasn't legislating in Austin, Representative McDonald worked as an area supervisor with the U.S. Department of Agriculture's Bureau of Agricultural Economics. He claimed his hobby was "collecting post-cards." Mrs. McDonald displays the fixed glare of a concerned young mother as she watches her offspring in the governor's arms. Is she worried that the baby will ruin the photo or that the governor will drop the baby?

Bryan, Texas, with Representative and Mrs. W. T. McDonald, fall 1940. (Texas State Library and Archives Commission #1976/8-393)

Governor O'Daniel posed with Representative Roger A. Knight, a teacher, and his fashionable wife on the porch of their home in Madisonville, the county seat of Madison County near Houston. Although O'Daniel proclaimed that he wanted to make his trip without appearances or speeches, the citizens of Madisonville couldn't help themselves. O'Daniel paraded through downtown in a Ford fire truck, accompanied by Representative Knight and Senator Clem Fain Jr., while the townsfolk looked on and scratched.

Madisonville, Texas, with Representative and Mrs. Roger A. Knight, fall 1940. (Texas State Library and Archives Commission #1976/8-395, #1976/8-401)

Livingston, Texas, with Representative E. A. Coker and family, fall 1940. (Texas State Library and Archives Commission #1976/8-407)

Seventy-five miles north of Houston, Livingston was a boomtown in 1940 thanks to the discovery of oil eight years earlier in the nearby Livingston field. The well-groomed sons of Representative Coker, an attorney, wear the same style clothing, perhaps made by Mrs. Coker using the same pattern, as was common at the time. Perhaps Governor O'Daniel told the boys stories about his own children, like the one he shared with his radio audience one Easter Sunday morning when he informed his listeners that his college-aged children—Pat, Mike, and Molly—had "started chasing bunnies all over the Mansion grounds before the company arrived and found just oodles and oodles of brightly colored Easter eggs." Mrs. O'Daniel does not seem to approve of the Cokers' dog.

Austin, Texas, with Representative Joe Carrington and wife, Senator J. Houghton Brownlee and wife, Pat O'Daniel, and others, fall 1940. (Texas State Library and Archives Commission #1976/8-409, #1976/8-413)

In Austin, Texas, Governor O'Daniel avoided posing at the University of Texas, the state Capitol, or any other noted landmark. Instead, the governor put on his boots and visited the home of Representative Joe C. Carrington, a well-known insurance carrier for Texas trucking companies. "In these days of modern ways there may be some folks who think that we are much smarter than folks were years ago," Governor O'Daniel said for the benefit of his radio audience. "Maybe yes, maybe no . . . but regardless of the great inventions and new methods, and styles, we still have to get the milk from the cow before we put it in the can." O'Daniel proved his point by milking one of Representative Carrington's cows, this despite the fact that O'Daniel once claimed that the farm chore he hated most was milking. Houghton Brownlee, who joined the O'Daniels and the Carrington family at their home, was an attorney and rancher and, in the Texas Senate, chairman of the powerful Highways and Motor Traffic Committee.

Representative Rae Files was one of two women to serve in the Forty-seventh Legislature's House of Representatives (no women served in the Senate). An unmarried teacher from Waxahachie, she came under attack from her fellow legislators when she criticized Governor O'Daniel for criticizing the performance of her fellow representatives. "I have never and I never will willingly let anyone make disparaging remarks about this Legislature," she declared from the floor of the House of Representatives in a speech that the press described as "level-spoken." "I know that we have good, bad, and indifferent people here just as we have the good, bad, and indifferent people in any community in the United States. But we have a larger percentage of good than in any group this size anywhere else . . . My loyalty, every ounce of it, is with my colleagues. My so-called outburst was for you. It might be called my parting gift to my friends in the Legislature because I love you very much and I know you've done a heck of a good job in spite of what anyone else says."

Waxahachie, Texas, with Representative Rae Files, fall 1940. (Texas State Library and Archives Commission #1976/8-423)

Rainbow, Texas, with young members of Senator Vernon Lemens's family, fall 1940. (Texas State Library and Archives Commission #1976/8-426)

Before he started out on his statewide photo odyssey, Governor O'Daniel told his radio audience, "I want to bounce [the legislators'] babies on my knee, meet their mother and dad, or their grandmother and grand-dad, see how their corn and potatoes are turning out, and learn to know them as they are, in their own homes." Here in Rainbow, Texas, near Waxahachie, at the home of Senator Vernon Lemens, the governor had his knees full of babies. Forty-year-old Senator Lemens was first elected to the Texas House of Representatives in 1928, while still a law student at the University of Texas, Austin, and was elected to the Texas Senate in 1936. In the Lemens home, as in so many homes of the day, the radio was a major feature in the family living room.

There is a strong family resemblance between Representative Herbert Brawner, his wife, and their tall, well-groomed children as they pose in their unpretentious home in Joshua, a farming community in the Cross Timbers region of central Johnson County. The two youngest daughters wear clothes made of the same pattern, just as the two sons of Representative E. A. Coker do (p. 82). Representative Brawner, a farmer in the populist mode, opposed large corporations muscling out the family farm. In the legislature, Rep. Brawner worked on a bill for a graduated land tax, claiming, "It will tend to keep the big fellow from gobbling up the little fellow's land."

Joshua, Texas, with Representative Herbert Brawner and family, fall 1940. (Texas State Library and Archives Commission #1976/8-431)

*Weatherford, Texas, with Rep-
resentative Arthur Cato, fall
1940. (Texas State Library
and Archives Commission
#1976/8-433)*

A large crowd gathered to hear Representative Arthur Cato and Governor O'Daniel on the square of the Parker County Courthouse in Weatherford, thirty miles west of Forth Worth. A former frontier settlement, Weatherford suffered Indian raids into the early 1870s.

When Governor O'Daniel visited the town, drivers pulled their cars up as close to the action as possible. As the Forty-seventh Legislature extended its session in part to prevent Pappy from campaigning for U.S. senator, it was Representative Cato, a druggist, who declared, "My county is a Pappy county and they want the Legislature to go home."

 **Driving across the state,** photographer Joe Tisdale couldn't resist taking this shot of cotton pickers in a field somewhere between Terrell and Rockwall. It is impossible to know why he took this picture. For whatever reason, this image of hands at work in a cotton field is as timeless as it is arresting. It is one of the photos most requested from the Department of Public Safety collection at the Texas State Library and Archives.

Between Terrell and Rock-
wall, Texas, fall 1940.
(Texas State Library and
Archives Commission
#1976/8-459)

From the Governor's Mansion in Austin, O'Daniel told his radio listeners on September 8, 1940, "Let's rejoice with all the boys and girls who are starting out to school this month, with a smile on their faces and a song in their hearts because—Happy Days Are Here Again." These Rockwall schoolchildren seem more curious than happy as they gather at the home of Senator Claude M. Isbell, an attorney. With a population of slightly more than 1,300, Rockwall was the county seat of Rockwall County, near the East Fork of the Trinity River. Senator Isbell worked hard to secure steady funding for Texas school districts before he retired from office on March 1, 1942.

Rockwall, Texas, at the home of Senator and Mrs. Claude Isbell, fall 1940. (Texas State Library and Archives Commission #1976/8-464)

*Terrell, Texas, at the home
of Representative and Mrs.
S. W. (Bill) Weatherford, fall
1940. (Texas State Library
and Archives Commission
#1976/8-468)*

A young girl presents a bouquet of roses to Governor O'Daniel at the home of Representative and Mrs. S. W. (Bill) Weatherford. Representative Weatherford resigned after the first called session of the Forty-seventh Legislature, but here Mrs. Weatherford and an older relative or family friend proudly look on through the screen door. The women are proud of the girl's good manners and her outfit, a suit made out of "Pass the Biscuits, Pappy" material that was produced and sold as part of Pappy O'Daniel's Hillbilly Flour marketing campaign.

"This idea of visiting folks in their own homes is an old custom that used to exist in this country, right after we took it over from the Indians," O'Daniel observed on the radio just before he set out on his statewide meet-and-greet, "and they tell me it was a mighty fine way of learning to know your neighbor better."

Chief Bronson Cooper Sylestine, the chief of the Alabama-Coushatta tribe, shakes hands with Governor O'Daniel at the Livingston home of Senator Clem Fain Jr. The Alabama-Coushatta tribe was the only tribe to remain in Texas after a policy of extermination and removal that was adopted by the Republic in 1836 and continued for the better part of one hundred years. Senator Fain served as Texas agent for the tribe and was instrumental in expanding their reservation. A few months before this visit, the Alabama-Coushattas ratified a constitution and a charter for the tribe.

Livingston, Texas, with Chief Bronson Cooper Sylestine at the home of Senator Clem Fain Jr., fall 1940. (Texas State Library and Archives Commission #1976/8-471)

Zavala, Texas, with Representative Ottis E. Lock, fall 1940. (Texas State Library and Archives Commission #1976/8-477, #1976/8-478)

Nothing could slow down Governor O'Daniel,

not even nightfall. In this photo (facing page), the governor addresses a large crowd gathered at the modest home of Representative Ottis Lock, a teacher in Zavala, Texas. Note the sedan converted into a pick-up in the foreground. Hard-pressed farmers were adept at converting automobiles into a variety of different kinds of vehicles, including tractors. The governor may have taken this opportunity to tell the people of Zavala that he believed America was becoming a more Christian civilization. As he told his radio audiences on September 29, 1940, "All men are inherently good—they only get out of the groove sometimes."

The simple home of Representative Washington M. Whitesides, a farmer, was probably similar to the homes of most rural Texans, O'Daniel's strongest supporters. Troup, a railroad town of about 3,000 residents in extreme southeastern Smith County, was fairly prosperous in the 1930s due to the productivity of the nearby East Texas oilfield. This is the kind of family that could most appreciate Governor O'Daniel's talks, which skillfully blended family, God, and politics. "Take the fourth commandment," Governor O'Daniel once explained to a group of supporters. "'Honor thy father and thy mother.' Doesn't that mean old-age pensions as plain as day?"

Troup, Texas, with Representative Washington M. Whitesides and his family, fall 1940. (Texas State Library and Archives Commission #1976/8-491)

Pickton, Texas, at the home of Representative Thomas Walters, fall 1940. (Texas State Library and Archives Commission #1976/8-501)

Representative Thomas Walters, a teacher, is not in this photograph. Perhaps he was not present, or perhaps he chose not to have his picture taken with Governor O'Daniel, whom he opposed on many issues. Representative Walters supported an increase in the natural resource tax, a position adamantly opposed by Governor O'Daniel and many of his pro-business supporters. Walters claimed that his proposal had a majority in the House, "But you've got to consider the Senate over there. They represent the aristocracy of the state." For whatever reason, Governor O'Daniel had his photo taken without Walters or his wife. Note the patched pants and the stained shirt on the older gentleman, presumably the father of Representative Walters. Even if they were not dressed up when the governor requested to take a photo, they could hardly turn him down.

Winnsboro, Texas, with Representative Joe W. Gandy and family, fall 1940. (Texas State Library and Archives Commission #1976/8-504, #1976/8-505)

 **Winnsboro,** home of Representative Joe Gandy, a newspaper writer and farmer, was particularly hard hit by the falling cotton prices of the Depression as people moved from towns to cities in search of work.

Representative Gandy said that his supporters were interested in putting the administration of old-age pensions in the hands of county commissioners, a position that did not gain much support. It is not possible to say why Joe Tisdale decided to photograph the worker on the Gandy ranch. Dressed in clean clothes for the governor's visit, this unidentified ranch hand represents the real Texas cowboy, a proud, hard-working man who could withstand the all-too-brutal Texas heat.

Dinner party in Paris,
Texas, with Senator and
Mrs. A. M. Aikin Jr., fall
1940. (Texas State Library
and Archives Commission
#1976/8-515, #1976/8-
514)

One of the longest-serving and most dedicated state senators, A. M. Aikin Jr. welcomed Pappy to his home in Paris, Texas, the seat of Lamar County. Pictured at a formal dinner, the thirty-three-year-old Senator Aikin is actually passing the biscuits to Governor Pappy while the family maid looks on. Aikin began his career in the legislature in 1933 and served for the next forty-six years. In the late 1960s, Senator Aikin was a strong supporter of the Texas State Archives current events photography program, which made it possible for the Archives to document state government activities in visual form.

Representative Garland, a farmer, smiles broadly as he stands alongside the governor surrounded by schoolchildren. Annona, named for an Indian girl, had a population of about 425 at the time. It appears that most of the town's citizens are gathered for the photo–graph. Looking at the feet of the children speaks volumes as to their economic condition. The crowd seems as ebullient as the governor, who announced over the radio at the beginning of his first term in office, "It looks like we are going to have just one big grand love feast at Austin and all over Texas for two years after the inauguration."

Annona, Texas, with Representative and Mrs. W. R. Garland and schoolchildren, fall 1940. (Texas State Library and Archives Commission #1976/8-516)

Harleton, Texas, with Representative Robert Avant, fall 1940. (Texas State Library and Archives Commission #1976/8-529)

This photo captures Governor O'Daniel, the award-winning salesman, making a pitch to Representative Robert Avant at his home in Harleton, Texas, in northwestern Harrison County. Although he swore he wouldn't talk politics on this trip, the governor might possibly be talking about his plans for funding pensions through a "transaction tax." As in several other photos, a possibly exhausted First Lady is caught with her eyes closed. Rumor had it that Mrs. O'Daniel was very weary of the bickering and turmoil in the Governor's Mansion and wanted to return to private life.

Governor O'Daniel was just as eager to pose with pets as he was to pose with babies. Here, he enjoys the dappled shade with a hunting dog at the home of Representative N. O. Burnaman, an editor and county judge, in Newton, the seat of Newton County. Representative Burnaman was a tireless advocate for what he termed the state's "200 poorer counties." In this image, the notoriously isolated Pappy looks comfortable, more at ease with a real dog than the "barking dogs," as he called his opponents in the legislature. During one radio broadcast, the governor recited a poem he had written about the legislative process entitled "The Barking Dog," which ended with the following verse:

> It takes a dog to fight a dog!
> Post that above your shelf;
> When canines come and snarl at you,
> Don't be a dog yourself.
> And later, when you're older grown,
> And petty men attack,
> Don't stoop to pick up stones to throw,
> Don't try to answer back;
> Just walk on and pay no heed
> To anything they say,
> And very soon they'll give it up
> And turn and run away.

Newton, Texas, at the home of Representative N. O. Burnaman, fall 1940. (Texas State Library and Archives Commission #1976/8-544)

For all his homespun airs, Governor O'Daniel never forgot that his true power lay in the microphone. "Yes, sir," Governor O'Daniel once told his radio audience, "just imagine that I am in your home today, and let us forget the cares and kicks of the week and just have a little friendly homey visit . . . yes, sir, be it only a microphone, it's home sweet home to me."

Representative Leslie Lowry, an insurance salesman, and other leading citizens of Beaumont, Texas, watch with interest as a reporter from radio station KRIC interviews the governor in what appears to be a live broadcast. Such remote broadcasts were rare for the time, when there were only 31 radio stations, and no television station, in the Lone Star State.

Beaumont, Texas, at the home of Representative Leslie P. Lowry, fall 1940. (Texas State Library and Archives Commission 1976/8-548-A)

Liberty, Texas, with Represen-
tative Marion Price Daniel
and his wife, Jean, fall 1940.
(Texas State Library and
Archives Commission
#1976/8-557)

Under the Spanish moss at their home in Liberty, Texas, thirty-year-old Representative Price Daniel holds hands with his wife, the former Jean Houston Baldwin, a great-great-granddaughter of Sam Houston. Representative Daniel would be elected speaker of the Texas House of Representatives in 1943. Three years later, he would become the youngest state attorney general in the United States. In 1952, he would be elected U.S. senator, only to give up his seat, declaring that he would "rather be governor of Texas than President of the United States." Senator Daniel was elected governor of Texas in 1956. Two years later, he ran for re-election against an aging O'Daniel, who told his radio audience, "Tomorrow you can vote for and elect W. Lee O'Daniel as governor of Texas or you can vote for my opponent and have integration, intermarriage, and ultimately a mongrelized race of people in Texas."

Senator Daniel defeated Senator O'Daniel and won a third term as governor in 1960. A devoted student of history, Governor Price Daniel did more than anyone else to promote the Texas State Library and Archives, and even helped design the Archives building. He later retired to a home in Liberty that he designed and built based on the original plans for the Governor's Mansion in Austin.

The sartorial splendor of Governor O'Daniel is reflected by this group of well-heeled legislators who fete the governor in Houston. In marked contrast to the poor, populist, and agricultural legislators photographed on this trip, the Houston group, all successful attorneys, represent the new face of Texas politics that was to emerge during World War II—wealthy, conservative, and industrial. But even these sophisticates were savvy enough to appreciate Governor O'Daniel's vote-getting power. Representative Joe E. Winfree introduced a resolution calling on O'Daniel to broadcast a program on Mother's Day 1939 from the House of Representatives. Standing at the podium in the House chamber, Governor O'Daniel cooed into the microphone, "Hello there mothers—you little sweetheart—How in the world are you anyhow?. . . you little bunch of sweetness." He then led Representative Winfree and the rest of his audience in singing "Let Me Call You Sweetheart."

Houston, Texas, with Representative William C. Montgomery seated in chair. On the sofa, from left to right, Representative George F. Howard, Senator Weaver Moore, Governor O'Daniel, and Representative Joe E. Winfree. Behind is Representative James Heflin, fall 1940. (Texas State Library and Archives Commission #1976/8-560)

In 1940, President Franklin Delano Roosevelt had been in office for eight years, yet most of America did not know that the president was a polio victim who had been wheelchair-bound from his youth. In contrast to FDR, who was reluctant to let voters know his true physical condition, Representative Markle, an attorney, stands proudly on his crutches between Governor O'Daniel and his wife on the porch of his Galveston home. Representative Markle was not afraid of losing votes by having such a picture taken. His constituents knew his condition, and supported him still.

Galveston, Texas, with Representative Donald Markle, fall 1940. (Texas State Library and Archives Commission #1976/8-570)

Angleton, Texas, with Representative and Mrs. Jimmy Phillips, fall 1940. (Texas State Library and Archives Commission #1976/8-571)

Representative Jimmy Phillips, a law student, and his wife pose in front of rented rooms in their hometown of Angleton, near the center of Brazoria County. If indeed Representative Phillips was renting rooms, he took no shame in it. An orphan, Phillips worked his way through law school and enjoyed a long and colorful career as a state legislator. In later years, Phillips took to wearing white suits and presenting supporters with two-dollar bills signed with his name.

*East Bernard, Texas, posing
with Representative
LaFayette L. Duckett and
other notables in a cotton
field (above) and on the
school parade grounds
(facing page), fall 1940.
(Texas State Library and
Archives Commission
#1976/8-574, #1976/
8-578)*

In the farming community of East Bernard in northeast Wharton County, Representative L. L. Duckett and other local luminaries literally stand in tall cotton with Governor O'Daniel. Governor O'Daniel never seemed to tire of talking about the bounty of Texas. Over the radio on Thanksgiving 1939, he described Texas as the place "where we can raise the finest oranges, grapefruit, apples, peaches . . . the biggest yams, finest potatoes, reddest tomatoes, greenest spinach, hottest onions, and bestest other varieties of garden truck." On the playing field at a local school, students and band members gaze upon their dapper governor from afar.

Representative C. S. McLellan and Governor O'Daniel addressed a crowd of students gathered in the town of Eagle Lake, fifty miles southwest of Houston in southeast Colorado County. Here photographer Joe Tisdale captures the face of small-town Texas youth, the youngest members of the greatest generation, perched on the edge of adulthood at the dawn of World War II. "Boys and girls take not this school year lightly," Governor O'Daniel told the students of Texas over the radio, "buckle down and apply yourselves to the tasks assigned to you . . . you are soldiers in the ranks of this great Democracy just as truly as the men in uniforms."

Eagle Lake, Texas, school-children and friends assemble to hear the governor, fall 1940. (Texas State Library and Archives Commission #1976/8-583)

Cuero, Texas, with represen-
tatives of the Cuero Turkey
Trot Association, fall 1940.
(Texas State Library and
Archives Commission
#1976/8-594)

Located in DeWitt County, Cuero was a center for turkey raising and processing and the site of the annual Turkey Trot parade. First celebrated in 1912 and named for the popular "turkey trot" dance of the period, the parade celebrated the annual November turkey drive, when turkeys from outlying farms were driven on foot to the Cuero market. As many as 20,000 live turkeys paraded in a single drive. The typically well-dressed Governor O'Daniel takes it in stride when asked to pose with a prize gobbler. The Cuero officials sitting beside him seem concerned about what the turkey, or the governor, will do.

At the home of Representative M. A. Hobbs, a farmer, Mrs. O'Daniel seems intrigued by the duckling in her husband's hands. Hallettsville, the seat of Lavaca County, was an agricultural community settled by Czech and German immigrants and was once a center for Texas socialism. The ardent anti-socialist Governor O'Daniel was decidedly pro-Texas. He once told his radio audience that he had driven through fields of Texas tomatoes one morning and later walked into a store, only to read "Made in New York" on a bottle of ketchup. "Make your own ketchup," he cried, "and put people to work."

Hallettsville, Texas, with Representative M. A. Hobbs and family, fall 1940. (Texas State Library and Archives Commission #1976/8-597)

Pleasanton, Texas, with Representative Magus F. Smith and family, fall 1940. (Texas State Library and Archives Commission #1976/8-617, #1976/8-618)

Representative Magus Smith, an attorney, and his family seem especially proud of their young barefoot son in the arms of the governor, who is holding a pair of aviator-style sunglasses in his right hand. Later, Joe Tisdale snapped a photo of the young adventurer headed down the porch stairs. It is not known whether the Smith baby took a tumble after the photograph was taken.

In Edinburg, the seat of Hidalgo County in deep south Texas, Senator Rogers Kelly sports a snakeskin belt as he passes the time with the governor and unidentified businessmen. A graduate of the University of the South with a law degree from the University of Colorado, thirty-seven-year-old Senator Kelly was the district attorney of Hidalgo County, an Episcopalian, and a proud member of the Phi Gamma Delta and Phi Gamma Phi fraternities. Governor O'Daniel, with his hair uncharacteristically out of place, displays the intense, hard-driving enthusiasm that earned him a fortune and the position of governor.

Edinburg, Texas, with Senator Rogers Kelly and associates, fall 1940. (Texas State Library and Archives Commission #1976/8-628)

Brownsville, Texas, with Representative Augustine Celaya, fall 1940. (Texas State Library and Archives Commission #1976/8-635)

Modeling *recuerdos* (souvenirs) from south of the border, Governor O'Daniel visits with Representative Augustine Celaya in Brownsville, Texas, in the Rio Grande Valley. As Governor O'Daniel once observed over the radio, "Agricultural experts say that the Rio Grande Valley of Texas is richer than the Valley of the Nile." Representative Celaya, a farmer and a real estate agent, was one of only two Mexican Americans to serve in the Texas House of Representatives from 1900 to 1953. Photographer Joe Tisdale used a vertical composition to capture the governor in all his glory. It is unknown what inspired Governor O'Daniel to flash a modified "scout's honor" sign while posing in his sombrero and serape.

Sheriff Arthur Knaggs was the law in Carrizo Springs, a farming and ranching community of about 2,100 and the seat of Dimmit County. First elected in 1936, Sheriff Knaggs was re-elected numerous times and served a total of eighteen years until his retirement from duty in 1955. Joining the sheriff and the governor in front of the Dimmit County courthouse is an unidentified local character.

Carrizo Springs, Texas,
with Sheriff Arthur Knaggs
and companion, fall 1940.
(Texas State Library and
Archives Commission
#1976/8-654)

Representative Clay Parker, an oilman, strikes a Texas Gothic pose as he stands next to his wife and the O'Daniels. Governor Pappy shared Representative Parker's reverence for the flag and once observed over the radio, "It is the humble prayer of this Governor that every school room in Texas will proudly display the United States flag every day and that each school will open each day with prayer."

Graham, Texas, with Representative and Mrs. Clay R. Parker, fall 1940. (Texas State Library and Archives Commission #1976/8-697)

*Winters, Texas, with Repre-
sentative W. H. Rampy and
family, fall 1940. (Texas
State Library and Archives
Commission #1976/8-704)*

The unflappable governor stands in a strong breeze outside the home of Representative Rampy, a garage man, in Winters, Texas. "Let me remind you that crops are good in Texas," the governor reported over the radio on October 20, 1940, soon after returning from his statewide trip, "folks are happy in Texas, democracy is functioning in Texas—Texas is not short on friendship and hospitality."

San Angelo, Texas, with
Senator Penrose B. Metcalfe
(back row, center) and oth-
ers, and Mertzon, Texas,
with Senator Metcalfe and
local officials, fall 1940.
(Texas State Library and
Archives Commission
#1976/8-705, #1976/8-
706)

Senator Penrose Metcalfe, an attorney and rancher, was chairman of the Military Affairs Committee in the Texas Senate, and a man who couldn't resist a good joke. "Listen to me friends, that is what really got me into trouble, associating with Senator Penrose Metcalfe," Governor O'Daniel told his listeners in radio land after returning from San Angelo. "Before we got to San Angelo, the Sheriff and his posse with their shotguns and pistols held us up at Mertzon, and put handcuffs on me and arrested me for lowering the dignity of the governor's office by being caught with their notorious Senator. . . . That was a close scrape." Senator Metcalfe raises his hands in surrender.

Pat O'Daniel (right) joins his parents and Representative and Mrs. R. Temple Dickson outside their home in Sweetwater, Texas. Photographer Tisdale chose to feature the wide-open West Texas sky in this portrait of the governor, who later told his radio audience, "Texas today is a veritable paradise."

Sweetwater, Texas, with Representative and Mrs. R. Temple Dickson, fall 1940. (Texas State Library and Archives Commission #1976/8-711)

Mission, Texas, with Senator Robert Allan Shivers and family, fall 1940. (Texas State Library and Archives Commission 1976/8-732)

Governor O'Daniel poses with the baby of thirty-two-year-old Senator Robert Allan Shivers and his wife, the former Maryalice Shary. A graduate of the University of Texas law school, Senator Shivers was first elected to the State Senate from Port Arthur in 1934. At age twenty-seven, he was the youngest member ever to sit in that body. After his marriage, Senator Shivers moved to Mission, where Mrs. Shivers's family had extensive interests in agriculture, banking, and real estate.

After serving in the military service in World War II, Shivers was elected lieutenant governor. He became governor of Texas after Governor Beauford H. Jester became the first governor to die in office. (Governor Jester succumbed to a heart attack, reportedly after overexerting himself with a female companion.) Shivers served as governor for the next seven and a half years. A strong pro-business, pro-segregation Republican-sympathizing conservative in the mold of Governor O'Daniel, Shivers led Texas in breaking away from the national Democratic party and delivering the state's electoral votes to Republican presidential nominee Dwight D. Eisenhower in 1952. He retired from politics in 1957, served on the Board of Regents of the University of Texas for many years, and later donated his historic home in Austin to the University.

Mrs. O'Daniel brought a group of orphans to the Governor's Mansion to spend Christmas week, 1940. Over the radio on December 15, 1940, Governor O'Daniel invited others to follow her example. "They are nice clean wholesome little boys and girls with all the life and fun and hope and aspirations of other little boys and girls who do have homes," the governor assured his listeners. "Pick out the boy or girl you want, any age you like, and be their Christmas Daddy or the Christmas Mother for all of Christmas week this year, and then take them back the following Sunday. . . May I also add, that if any colored families desire to share in this plan, you can go to the State Colored Orphans' Home in Gilmer and get you a little colored boy or girl to spend Christmas with you in your home."

Though he appreciated the children's company, Governor O'Daniel had vetoed additional funding for orphanages in 1939.

*Texas State School, Mrs.
O'Daniel with orphans,
December 17, 1940. (Texas
State Library and Archives
Commission #1976/8-114)*

*Austin, Texas, vendor in
front of the State Capitol,
January 21, 1941. (Texas
State Library and Archives
Commission #1976/8-89)*

With the Capitol building in the background, this vendor and a few young Texans look forward to the second inauguration of Governor Pappy O'Daniel on January 21, 1941. Included in the gubernatorial memorabilia are rabbits' feet and mini flour sacks.

"We want you to know that EVERYBODY is invited to the inauguration," Governor O'Daniel announced over the radio on January 19, 1941, "and to the big FREE BARBECUE immediately following the Inauguration ceremonies."

The vendor expected a big crowd.

Kerrville, Texas, with son
Pat O'Daniel and others,
January 18, 1941. (Texas
State Library and Archives
Commission #1976/8-159,
#1976/8-166)

A few days before the inaugural barbecue on the grounds of the Governor's Mansion in Austin, Governor O'Daniel traveled to Kerrville to kill a buffalo for the good people of Texas. In describing the adventure to his radio audience, Governor O'Daniel claimed that he "shouldered the old musket" and "went out west to the beautiful country around Kerrville and there found a fine herd of buffalo on the Schreiner Ranch." With daring and skill and a half-dozen well-armed assistants, O'Daniel succeeded "in picking out the finest buffalo in the herd and causing him to bite the dust." Over the radio, the governor invited everyone to come to Austin and "taste some of this deliciously barbecued buffalo, brought in by the skilled hands and steady nerve of your governor in possibly the last great wild buffalo hunt of this century." Motion pictures of the event shot by the Department of Public Safety show that Governor Pappy didn't really "hunt" the buffalo as much as he walked up to it in a pen and shot it at point-blank range. The shot did not kill the buffalo, which groggily raised its shaggy head as the hunters struck their post-kill poses. It is not known why Governor O'Daniel later chose to rope his prey.

*Austin, Texas, with beef
before and during barbecu-
ing, January 1941. (Texas
State Library and Archives
Commission #1976/8-95,
#1976/8-66)*

Inaugural planners realized that one buffalo was not going to be enough to feed a crowd of 20,000. Here (facing page) Governor O'Daniel poses with beef delivered in a truck bearing the sign, "Donated by Fort Worth Friends of Governor W. Lee O'Daniel and Family Inauguration and Barbecue Austin, Texas, January 21st—1941." Molly O'Daniel, wearing sunglasses in the left of the picture (below), inspected one of the barbecue pits that were dug around the Governor's Mansion to prepare 6,000 pounds of beef, as well as mutton, chicken, hot dogs, turkey, and one buffalo.

Austin, Texas, inauguration
preparation, January 20,
1941. (Texas State Library
and Archives Commission
(#1976/8-70, #1976/8-67)

In the hours before his inauguration,
Governor O'Daniel helped carve up the inaugural barbecue.
Sides included 800 pounds of coffee, 1,500 pounds of onions,
1,000 pounds of potato chips, a boxcar-load of Rio Grande grapefruit,
500 dozen lemons for lemonade, 1,000 pounds of potato salad, and 3,500
loaves of bread. Hundreds of volunteers helped prepare the barbecue, including
these women who are busy slicing some 1,300 pickles.

In contrast to his first inauguration held at the University of Texas Memorial Stadium, Governor O'Daniel's second inauguration took place on the south steps of the Capitol. In this photograph, daughter Molly helps her father look presentable while her brother Pat, at far right, checks his camera. Governor O'Daniel appreciated his daughter's gesture, and once penned a song entitled, "The Boy Who Never Gets Too Big to Comb His Mother's Hair."

Austin, Texas, inauguration of Texas governor, January 21, 1941. (Courtesy of Chuck Bailey)

Austin, Texas, inauguration
barbecue, January 21, 1941.
(Texas State Library and
Archives Commission
#1976/8-88, #1976/8-82)

By the end of the Great Depression, everyone in Texas appreciated free chow.

Austin, Texas, inauguration
barbecue, January 21, 1941.
(Texas State Library and
Archives Commission
#1976/8-80, #1976/8-84)

An estimated 20,000 people lined up at the Governor's Mansion for a taste of inaugural barbecue. Note the lack of garbage cans on the littered grounds as seen from above.

With General Andrew Jackson Houston, April 21, 1941. (Texas State Library and Archives Commission #1976/8-189, #1976/8-192)

Governor W. Lee O'Daniel arrived unannounced at the home of General Andrew Jackson Houston on April 21, 1941. The home was located within sight of the San Jacinto Battleground Historical State Park, commemorating the place where General Andrew Jackson Houston's father, the legendary General Sam Houston, had defeated the army of Mexico to win Texas independence. Governor O'Daniel told the eighty-seven-year-old gentleman that he had been appointed U.S. Senator to complete the term of Senator Morris Sheppard, who had died in office. "Just as I broke the news to him of his appointment," Governor O'Daniel later told his radio audience, "the sun suddenly shot through the dark rain cloud in such a fashion that it appeared dazzling. I said: 'General, do you know what caused that sun to suddenly burst through those dark and heavy clouds? It appears to me as if our great and good loving God had just spread the clouds apart so the spirit of your illustrious father could smile down upon his son in this particular scene and see the big smile on your face.'" According to Houston's daughters, the elderly Republican did indeed laugh out loud when Governor O'Daniel told him the news.

After Governor O'Daniel announced his candidacy for the U.S. Senate in May 1941, his daughter, Molly, congratulated him with a kiss on the cheek. Congressman Lyndon Baines Johnson ultimately lost the race to Governor Pappy, the only electoral contest the future president ever lost.

Austin, Texas, with Molly
O'Daniel, May 1941.
(Texas State Library and
Archives Commission
#1976/8-248)

Waco, Texas, on the cam-
paign trail for U.S. Senate,
July 2, 1941. (Texas State
Library and Archives Com-
mission #1976/8-255,
#1976/8-264)

On June 30, 1941, Governor O'Daniel explained to his radio audience that, because the legislature had stayed in session for so long, he would not be able to campaign for the U.S. Senate across the whole state. Instead, Governor O'Daniel invited all Texas to come to Waco on July 2 and warned, "I will attempt to boil the whole 30-day campaign down to one speech—and when I say boil it down, you can expect it to be hot, so HOT in fact it will not be broadcast."

At Waco, Governor O'Daniel appeared with his Hillbilly Boys on the same campaign truck that he had used in his second campaign for governor, the year before.

Waco, Texas, O'Daniel for U.S. Senate rally, July 2, 1941. (Texas State Library and Archives Commission #1976/8-258, #1976/8-259)

A driving rain shrank Governor O'Daniel's crowd in Waco from 5,500 to 500. Those who remained cheered their governor as he spoke for over an hour. He blasted his opponents in the race for the U.S. Senate seat in much the same language that he had used over the radio to characterize the voices of opposition as "the howlings of two or three wise-cracking political proselytizers polluting the place performing a personality piracy plot for the purpose of plucking personal publicity by the papers printing their prattle."

Everyone was having fun, including Pat and Molly, who joined their rain-soaked father beneath the faux capitol dome of his campaign truck.

Austin, Texas, the wedding of Molly O'Daniel, July 31, 1941. (Texas State Library and Archives Commission #1976/8-204, #1976/8-234)

Before he left for Washington, Senator-elect O'Daniel went on the air and announced the marriage of his daughter Molly to Jack Wrather Jr. of Tyler. "Molly has so many friends all over the state that she wants to invite all of them to be with her on that eventful evening and we are therefore extending an invitation to all of you folks everywhere to come to Molly's wedding here at the Mansion," the governor told his radio audience.

"July 31 at 8 o'clock in the evening . . . We would like to hear from all of you folks who will come so we can arrange to have enough of the wedding cake to go around."

While a select crowd attended the ceremony inside, an estimated 25,000 spectators accepted Governor Pappy's invitation and gathered on the lawn of the Mansion. They listened to loudspeakers as Molly and Jack took their vows. It was only the third wedding to be held in the Governor's Mansion. After the ceremony, all the well-wishers enjoyed fruit juice and wedding cake.

In one of the few shots in the DPS collection in which the governor is not spotlessly dressed, Governor O'Daniel drinks milk, eats chicken, and might just be ready to ask photographer Joe Tisdale to "please pass the biscuits." Looking back on his trips across the state, Governor O'Daniel recalled that one thing stood out most clearly in his mind. "Boy, oh boy," Governor O'Daniel told his radio friends. "I never saw so much fried chicken in all my life . . . If anybody asks me what is the leading industry in Texas I will say chicken raising . . . or chicken frying . . . or chicken eating."

On August 3, 1941, W. Lee O'Daniel broadcast to the people of Texas "by transcription," meaning his message had been previously recorded. The governor, who was in Washington, D.C., at the time, preparing to take his seat in the U.S. Senate, summed up his accomplishments for his radio audience and ended his final broadcast as governor with the following exhortation:

"May I urge that all of you go to the church of your choice today and every Sunday and take the little boys and girls along with you. Remember, as the twig is bent, the tree inclines . . . and a little child still leads us. This is Governor W. Lee O'Daniel of Texas speaking . . . Goodbye."

Austin, Texas. (Texas State Library and Archives Commission #1976/198-9)

Notes on Photos and Sources

Unless otherwise noted, photographs in the main body of the text are from the Archives Division of the Texas State Library, P.O. Box 12927, Austin, TX 78711-2927, (512) 463-5506. Copies of Texas State Library photographs are available from the Archives Division. When ordering copies of photos, please provide the photograph number as cited for each photograph.

Information about the location and history of Texas communities is from *The Handbook of Texas Online.* Information on the individual legislators comes from Sam H. Acheson, ed., *Texian Who's Who: A Biographical Dictionary of the State of Texas* (Dallas: The Texian Company, 1937); *The Handbook of Texas Online; The Members of the Texas Legislatures,* published by the Senate Engrossing and Enrolling and Senate Reproduction; *Roster and Standing Committees Forty-seventh Legislature, the Senate and House of Representatives* (Austin: Texas Legislative Service, 1941); and articles from the *Dallas Morning News* and other Texas publications provided in the database of the Texas Legislative Reference Library. All quotes from the radio speeches of Governor O'Daniel come from the Governor's Papers, W. Lee O'Daniel, the Texas State Library and Archives Commission.